Writing Grade 3

M000110925

Table of Contents

Writing Grade 3   CD-3718   Printed in the United States of America   ISBN 0-88724-436-X

A NOTE TO PARENTS AND TEACHERS

Children are natural storytellers. Most of them can hardly wait to recount their experiences to their teacher or friends. An important task of the parent and teacher is to turn these storytellers into story writers. Children who begin to write early become comfortable with the process. Writing becomes as natural as speaking. It is important to make writing a part of the daily schedule.

Many children find writing difficult because they do not understand how to write. They do not even know how to begin. Any writing activity must be modeled by the teacher several times before a child can grasp the concepts. To achieve the greatest affect, the activity should be conducted with a group. This allows the free exchange of ideas and prompts deeper thinking that will assist in better clarity and comprehension of the concepts. When the task is fully understood and mastered within groups, individual assignments become appropriate.

Writing is a process, and it takes time to develop ideas into a finished product. Neither the teacher nor student should expect a well designed story to emerge from an initial attempt. Teachers and students should look upon writing as a five step process. The first step is gathering ideas pertaining to the writing assignment. The second step is selecting and organizing those ideas into a rough draft. Third is the revising step to reorganize content and refine wording. The fourth step is editing (proofreading) for grammar, capitalization, and punctuation errors. Lastly, the paper is rewritten as a final copy. Remember to use these five steps to guide the writing process.

Students do willingly what they do well. Direct instruction, ample opportunities to practice skills, and exciting topics will support these storytellers in our quest to make them story writers.

About the author...

During her many years as an educator, **Rae Anne Roberson** has taught in elementary, junior and senior high, and university level settings. She is currently the Title 1 Instructional Facilitator in her school system and is helping to develop several innovative reading programs for "at risk" students in elementary schools. Rae Anne is very active as a presenter at workshops for teachers and parents. She was recently presented with the "Award for Literacy" for her school system. Certified in elementary and secondary education as well as reading specialist, Rae Anne holds an M.Ed. and is currently working toward her doctorate.

Senior Editors: Patricia Pedigo and Roger DeSanti
Production Supervisor: Homer Desrochers
Production: Arlene Evitts and Debra Ollier

Ready-To-Use Ideas and Activities

The activities in this book will help students master the basic skills necessary to become competent writers. Remember as you read through the activities listed below, and as you go through this book, that all children learn at their own rate. Although repetition is important, it is critical that we never lose sight of the fact that it is equally important to build children's self-esteem and self-confidence if we want them to become successful learners as well as good citizens.

If you are working with a child at home, try to set up a quiet comfortable environment where you will work. Make it a special time to which you each look forward. Do only a few activities at a time. Try to end each session on a positive note, and remember that fostering self-esteem and self-confidence are also critical to the learning process.

The back of this book has removable flash cards that will be great for use for basic skill and vocabulary enrichment activities. Pull the flash cards out and either cut them apart or, if you have access to a paper cutter, use that to cut the flash cards apart.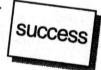

Following are checklists that students should use to help keep their sentence and paragraph writing on track.

Sentence Editing Checklist

Answer each question on this checklist either Yes or No. If your answer to any question is "No" or "I'm not sure," list that part of the report as a part that needs to be worked on.

Do most of your sentences say "who did what" and in that order?
❏ Yes ❏ No

Is every sentence complete?
❏ Yes ❏ No

Does every sentence begin with a capital letter and end with a period, question mark, or exclamation point?
❏ Yes ❏ No

Are all your verbs in the same tense, either present or past?
❏ Yes ❏ No

Are all your sentences in the third person (unless your assignment says that you can use first or second person)?
❏ Yes ❏ No

Paragraph Editing Checklist

Answer each question on this checklist either Yes or No. If your answer to any question is "No" or "I'm not sure," list that part of your paper as a part that needs to be worked on.

Does each paragraph have a topic sentence?
❏ Yes ❏ No

Are your supporting details convincing?
❏ Yes ❏ No

Are the supporting details in logical order?
❏ Yes ❏ No

Have you tried to add special details or lively quotes?
❏ Yes ❏ No

Did you take out all dull or unnecessary information?
❏ Yes ❏ No

Have you removed sentences that don't belong with the others?
❏ Yes ❏ No

Ready-To-Use Ideas and Activities

Basic Outline Format
Title

    I.   Opening
    II.   First Main Point or Idea
         A.   Supporting detail
         B.   More supporting detail
    III.   Next Main Point or Idea
         A.   Supporting detail
         B.   More supporting detail
         C.   More supporting detail
    IV.   Last Main Point or Idea
         A.   Supporting detail
         B.   More supporting detail
         C.   More supporting detail
    V.   Conclusion

Reasons For Writing

Expose your students to the many types of writing that are out in the world. Newspapers, magazines, advertisements, weather forecasts, recipes, poems, automotive manuals, short stories, novels, personal letters, and more. Once students are exposed to the many forms of writing, chances are very good that interests will peak and writing will become more enjoyable.

Creative Writing
Ask students to read an article in the newspaper. Once read, have students rewrite the article with a different ending. This exercise is extremely effective in helping students understand the importance of supporting details. Other great creative writing activities include:
- Writing letters to the school principal
- Responding to an editorial in the newspaper
- Interviewing a family member
- Writing directions for assembling a kite
- Writing a recipe for a favorite food
- Writing a T.V. script

CD-3718

Name _____

September

Write a story about things you do during September.

October

Write a story about things you do during October.

_____

_____

_____

_____

_____

_____

_____

_____

_____

_____

_____

_____

_____

November

Write a story about things you do during November.

December

Write a story about things you do during December.

_____

_____

_____

_____

_____

_____

_____

_____

_____

_____

_____

_____

_____

_____

January

Write a story about things you do during January.

February

Write a story about things you do during February.

_____

_____

_____

_____

_____

_____

_____

_____

_____

_____

_____

_____

_____

March

Write a story about things you do during March.

_____

_____

_____

_____

_____

_____

_____

_____

_____

_____

_____

_____

_____

April

Write a story about things you do during April.

_____

_____

_____

_____

_____

_____

_____

_____

_____

_____

_____

_____

_____

_____

_____

May

Write a story about things you do during May.

_____

_____

_____

_____

_____

_____

_____

_____

_____

_____

_____

_____

_____

June

Write a story about things you do during June.

_____

_____

_____

_____

_____

_____

_____

_____

_____

_____

_____

_____

_____

July

Write a story about things you do during July.

_____

_____

_____

_____

_____

_____

_____

_____

_____

_____

_____

_____

_____

_____

_____

August

Write a story about things you do during August.

_____

_____

_____

_____

_____

_____

_____

_____

_____

_____

_____

_____

_____

_____

Stories have a beginning, a middle, and an end.

Finish this story. Add a middle and an end. Be sure to use capitals and periods.

<u>A New Girl</u>

Susan sat down in her desk at school. She started to put her books away. A new student walked into the classroom. She sat in the desk next to Susan. The new student looked very frightened. Susan

_____

_____

_____

_____

_____

_____

_____

_____

_____

_____

_____

_____

_____

_____

_____

| Stories have a beginning, a middle, and an end. |

Finish this story. Add a middle and an end. Be sure to use capitals and periods.

The Birthday

"Happy birthday!" said Eric's mom and dad. "We have decided that you may have a pet as your birthday present. Let's go to the pet store."

"Great!" said Eric. "I know just the pet I would like to have."

_____

_____

_____

_____

_____

_____

_____

_____

_____

_____

_____

_____

_____

_____

_____

_____

Stories have a beginning, a middle, and an end.

Finish this story. Add a middle and an end. Be sure to use capitals and periods.

<u>A Swimming Race</u>

Jim loves to swim. He and his friends go swimming in the lake every day. Everyone agrees that Jim and Ron are the best swimmers. One day Jim and Ron decided to have a race across the lake. They stood on the dock and dove in at the same time.

_____

_____

_____

_____

_____

_____

_____

_____

_____

_____

_____

_____

_____

_____

_____

_____

_____

| Stories have a beginning, a middle, and an end. |

Finish this story. Add a middle and an end. Be sure to use capitals and periods.

<u>Mason</u>

Pam's dog Mason loved to chase cats. One morning when they were out for a walk a big white cat raced across their path. Mason barked at the cat. Pam could feel him pull on his leash. "No, Mason! Stop!" cried Pam, but it was too late.

_____

_____

_____

_____

_____

_____

_____

_____

_____

_____

_____

_____

_____

_____

_____

_____

_____

_____

| Stories have a beginning, a middle, and an end. |

Finish this story. Add a middle and an end. Be sure to use capitals and periods.

<u>The Storm</u>

The weatherman said that a terrible storm would be coming to our city. Dark clouds began to turn the sky black. Thunder boomed and lightning flashed. Rain began to pour on the roof. There was a streak of lightning and the lights went out. Our house was in total darkness.

_____
_____
_____
_____
_____
_____
_____
_____
_____
_____
_____
_____
_____
_____
_____
_____

| Stories have a beginning, a middle, and an end. |

Write five more words about the picture in the word box. Use the words to write
a story. Be sure to use capitals and periods. Think of a title for your story.

─────────────── Things To Think About ───────────────
Who is this story about? Where does this story take place? How does
this story begin? What happens next? How will you make this story end?

Word Box

children   _____

noisy   _____

yellow   _____

_____   _____

_____

_____

_____

_____

_____

_____

_____

_____

_____

Stories have a beginning, a middle, and an end.

Write five more words about the picture in the word box. Use the words to write a story. Be sure to use capitals and periods. Think of a title for your story.

―――――― Things To Think About ――――――
Who is this story about? Where does this story take place? How does this story begin? What happens next? How will you make this story end?

Word Box

trick-or-treat   _____

pumpkin   _____

scary   _____

_____   _____

_____

_____

_____

_____

_____

_____

_____

_____

_____

Stories have a beginning, a middle, and an end.

Write five more words about the picture in the word box. Use the words to write a story. Be sure to use capitals and periods. Think of a title for your story.

—————————— **Things To Think About** ——————————
Who is this story about? Where does this story take place? How does this story begin? What happens next? How will you make this story end?

Word Box

Eskimo	_____
snow	_____
ice hole	_____
_____	_____

_____

_____

_____

_____

_____

_____

_____

_____

_____

_____

Stories have a beginning, a middle, and an end.

Write five more words about the picture in the word box. Use the words to write
a story. Be sure to use capitals and periods. Think of a title for your story.

─── Things To Think About ───
**Who is this story about? Where does this story take place? How does
this story begin? What happens next? How will you make this story end?**

Word Box

bird	_____
crack	_____
spring	_____
_____	_____

_____

_____

_____

_____

_____

_____

_____

_____

_____

_____

Stories have a beginning, a middle, and an end.

Write five more words about the picture in the word box. Use the words to write a story. Be sure to use capitals and periods. Think of a title for your story.

— Things To Think About —
Who is this story about? Where does this story take place? How does this story begin? What happens next? How will you make this story end?

Word Box

crunchy _____

warm _____

beverage _____

_____ _____

_____

_____
_____
_____
_____
_____
_____
_____
_____

Stories have a beginning, a middle, and an end.

Write five more words about the picture in the word box. Use the words to write a story. Be sure to use capitals and periods. Think of a title for your story.

—————— Things To Think About ——————
Who is this story about? Where does this story take place? How does this story begin? What happens next? How will you make this story end?

Word Box

ocean _____

treasure chest _____

blue _____

_____ _____

_____

_____

_____

_____

_____

_____

_____

_____

_____

_____

Stories have a beginning, a middle, and an end.

Write five more words about the picture in the word box. Use the words to write a story. Be sure to use capitals and periods. Think of a title for your story.

─────────────── Things To Think About ───────────────
Who is this story about? Where does this story take place? How does this story begin? What happens next? How will you make this story end?

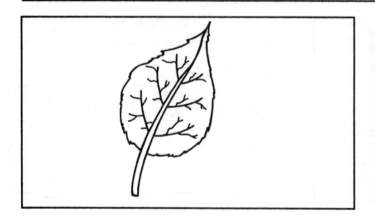

Word Box

autumn	_____
orange	_____
yellow	_____
_____	_____

_____

_____

_____

_____

_____

_____

_____

_____

_____

_____

_____

Name _____

| Stories have a beginning, a middle, and an end. |

Finish the story web. Use the words in the web to write a story about
the picture. Be sure to use capitals and periods. Think of a title for your story.

| ——————————————— Things To Think About ——————————————— |
| Who is this story about? Where does this story take place? How does
this story begin? What happens next? How will you make this story end? |

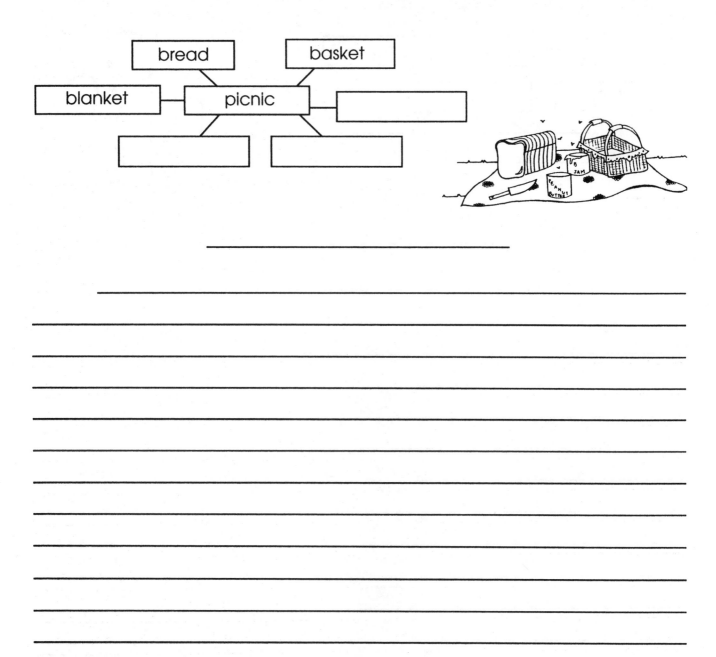

_____

_____

_____

_____

_____

_____

_____

_____

_____

_____

Stories have a beginning, a middle, and an end.

Finish the story web. Use the words in the web to write a story about the picture. Be sure to use capitals and periods. Think of a title for your story.

Things To Think About
Who is this story about? Where does this story take place? How does this story begin? What happens next? How will you make this story end?

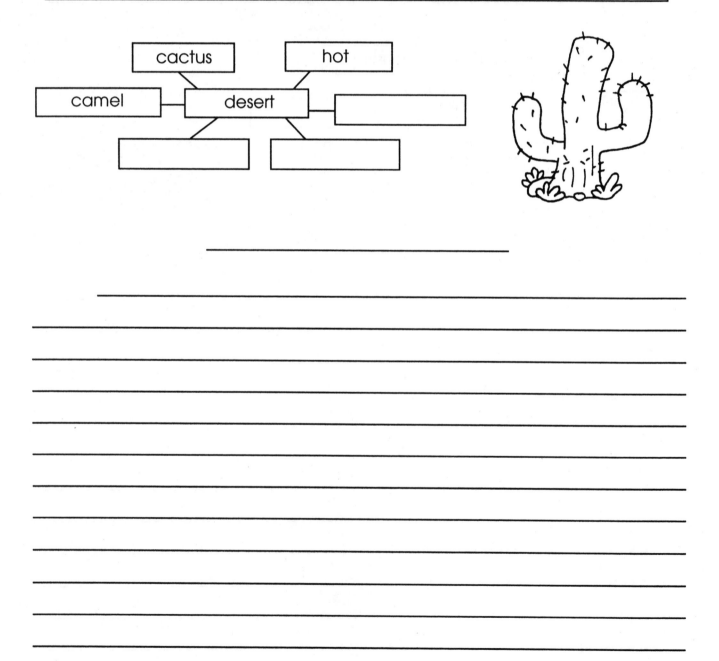

_____

_____

_____

_____

_____

_____

_____

_____

_____

_____

_____

_____

Stories have a beginning, a middle, and an end.

Finish the story web. Use the words in the web to write a story about the picture. Be sure to use capitals and periods. Think of a title for your story.

── Things To Think About ──
Who is this story about? Where does this story take place? How does this story begin? What happens next? How will you make this story end?

scarf   skis

snow   skiing   [   ]

[   ]   [   ]

_____

_____

_____

_____

_____

_____

_____

_____

_____

_____

Stories have a beginning, a middle, and an end.

Finish the story web. Use the words in the web to write a story about
the picture. Be sure to use capitals and periods. Think of a title for your story.

—— Things To Think About ——
Who is this story about? Where does this story take place? How does
this story begin? What happens next? How will you make this story end?

_____

_____

_____

_____

_____

_____

_____

_____

_____

_____

| Stories have a beginning, a middle, and an end. |

Finish the story web. Use the words in the web to write a story about the picture. Be sure to use capitals and periods. Think of a title for your story.

──────── Things To Think About ────────
Who is this story about? Where does this story take place? How does this story begin? What happens next? How will you make this story end?

_____

_____

_____

_____

_____

_____

_____

_____

_____

_____

_____

_____

Stories have a beginning, a middle, and an end.

Finish the story web. Use the words in the web to write a story about the picture. Be sure to use capitals and periods. Think of a title for your story.

Things To Think About
Who is this story about? Where does this story take place? How does this story begin? What happens next? How will you make this story end?

swim

pool

happy

water park

_____

_____

_____

_____

_____

_____

_____

_____

_____

_____

_____

Name _____ Skill: Constructing Stories

| Stories have a beginning, a middle, and an end. |

Write 5 sentences about this picture. Use the boxes at the end of each line to number your sentences in story order. Write your story. Title the story. Be sure to use capitals and periods.

1. _____ ☐

2. _____ ☐

3. _____ ☐

4. _____ ☐

5. _____ ☐

—— Things To Think About ——
Who is this story about? Where does this story take place? How does this story begin? What happens next? How will you make this story end?

_____

_____

_____

_____

_____

_____

_____

_____

_____

_____

Stories have a beginning, a middle, and an end.

Write 5 sentences about this picture. Use the boxes at the end of each line to number your sentences in story order. Write your story. Title the story. Be sure to use capitals and periods.

1. _____ ☐

2. _____ ☐

3. _____ ☐

4. _____ ☐

5. _____ ☐

───────────── Things To Think About ─────────────
Who is this story about? Where does this story take place? How does this story begin? What happens next? How will you make this story end?

_____

_____

_____

_____

_____

_____

_____

_____

_____

_____

_____

Name _____ Skill: Constructing Stories

> Stories have a beginning, a middle, and an end.

Write 5 sentences about this picture. Use the boxes at the end of each line to
number your sentences in story order. Write your story. Title the story. Be sure
to use capitals and periods.

1. _____ ☐

2. _____ ☐

3. _____ ☐

4. _____ ☐

5. _____ ☐

> — Things To Think About —
> Who is this story about? Where does this story take place? How does
> this story begin? What happens next? How will you make this story end?

_____

_____

_____

_____

_____

_____

_____

_____

_____

| Stories have a beginning, a middle, and an end. |

Write 5 sentences about this picture. Use the boxes at the end of each line to number your sentences in story order. Write your story. Title the story. Be sure to use capitals and periods.

1. _____ ☐
2. _____ ☐
3. _____ ☐
4. _____ ☐
5. _____ ☐

──── Things To Think About ────
Who is this story about? Where does this story take place? How does this story begin? What happens next? How will you make this story end?

_____

_____

_____

_____

_____

_____

_____

_____

_____

_____

_____

Stories have a beginning, a middle, and an end.

Write 5 sentences about this picture. Use the boxes at the end of each line to number your sentences in story order. Write your story. Title the story. Be sure to use capitals and periods.

1. _____ ☐

2. _____ ☐

3. _____ ☐

4. _____ ☐

5. _____ ☐

—— Things To Think About ——
Who is this story about? Where does this story take place? How does this story begin? What happens next? How will you make this story end?

_____

_____
_____
_____
_____
_____
_____
_____
_____
_____
_____

| Stories have a beginning, a middle, and an end. |

Write 5 sentences about this picture. Use the boxes at the end of each line to number your sentences in story order. Write your story. Title the story. Be sure to use capitals and periods.

1. _____ ☐
2. _____ ☐
3. _____ ☐
4. _____ ☐
5. _____ ☐

─── **Things To Think About** ───
Who is this story about? Where does this story take place? How does this story begin? What happens next? How will you make this story end?

_____

_____

_____

_____

_____

_____

_____

_____

_____

_____

Stories have a beginning, a middle, and an end.

Write a story about the picture. Add your own ending. Be sure to use capitals and periods. Title your story.

Things To Think About
Who is this story about? Where does this story take place? How does this story begin? What happens next? How will you make this story end?

_____

_____

_____

_____

_____

_____

_____

_____

_____

_____

_____

_____

Stories have a beginning, a middle, and an end.

Write a story about the picture. Add your own ending. Be sure to use capitals and periods. Title your story.

Things To Think About

Who is this story about? Where does this story take place? How does this story begin? What happens next? How will you make this story end?

_____

_____

_____

_____

_____

_____

_____

_____

_____

_____

_____

_____

_____

_____

_____

| Stories have a beginning, a middle, and an end. |

Write a story about the picture. Add your own ending. Be sure to use capitals and periods. Title your story.

Things To Think About
Who is this story about? Where does this story take place? How does this story begin? What happens next? How will you make this story end?

_____

_____

_____

_____

_____

_____

_____

_____

_____

_____

_____

_____

_____

_____

_____

_____

_____

_____

| Stories have a beginning, a middle, and an end. |

Write a story about the picture. Add your own ending. Be sure to use capitals and periods. Title your story.

| ——————————————— Things To Think About ——————————————— |
| Who is this story about? Where does this story take place? How does this story begin? What happens next? How will you make this story end? |

_____

_____

_____

_____

_____

_____

_____

_____

_____

_____

_____

_____

Stories have a beginning, a middle, and an end.

Write a story about the picture. Add your own ending. Be sure to use capitals and periods. Title your story.

Things To Think About
Who is this story about? Where does this story take place? How does this story begin? What happens next? How will you make this story end?

_____

_____

_____

_____

_____

_____

_____

_____

_____

_____

_____

_____

_____

_____

_____

Name _____

Skill: Writing Stories

| Stories have a beginning, a middle, and an end. |

Write a story about the picture. Add your own ending. Be sure to use capitals and periods. Title your story.

─── **Things To Think About** ───
Who is this story about? Where does this story take place? How does this story begin? What happens next? How will you make this story end?

_____

_____
_____
_____
_____
_____
_____
_____
_____
_____
_____
_____
_____
_____

© 1996 Kelley Wingate Publications   42   CD-3718

A paragraph contains a main idea and supporting details.

Every paragraph has one main idea. The main idea is called the **topic sentence**. It is usually the first sentence in the paragraph. The other sentences are **details** that tell more about the main idea. The last sentence retells the main idea.

1. Read the main idea and details listed below.

Title of paragraph: <u>**My Mom**</u>

Main Idea: My mom is the best!

Details: 1. She gives me hugs and kisses.
          2. She helps me with my homework.
          3. She cooks great dinners.
          4. She takes me shopping.

Retell Main Idea: I think my mom is wonderful.

2. Use these sentences to write a paragraph. Write the main idea, add the details, then retell the main idea. Indent the first sentence. Use capitals and periods. Remember to give the paragraph a title.

_____

_____

_____

_____

_____

_____

_____

_____

_____

A paragraph contains a main idea and supporting details.

Every paragraph has one main idea. The main idea is called the **topic sentence**. It is usually the first sentence in the paragraph. The other sentences are **details** that tell more about the main idea. The last sentence retells the main idea.

1. Read the main idea and details listed below.

Title of paragraph: <u>Washing My Hair</u>

Main Idea: I wash my hair at least four times a week.

Details:
1. I get in the shower.
2. I wet my hair.
3. I pour shampoo on my head.
4. I rinse my hair well.

Retell Main Idea: Now I have clean hair.

2. Use these sentences to write a paragraph. Write the main idea, add the details, then retell the main idea. Indent the first sentence. Use capitals and periods. Remember to give the paragraph a title.

_____

_____

_____

_____

_____

_____

_____

_____

_____

A paragraph contains a main idea and supporting details.

Every paragraph has one main idea. The main idea is called the **topic sentence**. It is usually the first sentence in the paragraph. The other sentences are **details** that tell more about the main idea. The last sentence retells the main idea.

1. Read the title and main idea of the paragraph. Write your own details.

Title of paragraph: <u>Making Toast</u>

Main Idea: Toast is easy to make.

Details:
1. _____
2. _____
3. _____
4. _____

Retell Main Idea: It is not hard to make toast. _____

2. Use these sentences to write a paragraph. Write the main idea, add the details, then retell the main idea. Indent the first sentence. Use capitals and periods. Remember to give the paragraph a title.

_____

_____

_____

_____

_____

_____

_____

_____

_____

A paragraph contains a main idea and supporting details.

Every paragraph has one main idea. The main idea is called the **topic sentence**. It is usually the first sentence in the paragraph. The other sentences are **details** that tell more about the main idea. The last sentence retells the main idea.

1. Read the title and main idea of the paragraph. Write your own details.

Title of paragraph: <u>**Playing Baseball**</u>

Main Idea: Baseball is an exciting game to play!

Details: 1. _____
                        2. _____
                        3. _____
                        4. _____

Retell Main Idea: Now you see why I love baseball.
_____

2. Use these sentences to write a paragraph. Write the main idea, add the details, then retell the main idea. Indent the first sentence. Use capitals and periods. Remember to give the paragraph a title.

                    _____

_____

_____

_____

_____

_____

_____

_____

_____

Name _____ Skill: Writing Paragraphs

A paragraph contains a main idea and supporting details.

Every paragraph has one main idea. The main idea is called the **topic sentence**. It is usually the first sentence in the paragraph. The other sentences are **details** that tell more about the main idea. The last sentence retells the main idea.

1. Read the title and main idea of the paragraph. Write your own details.

Title of paragraph: <u>**Birthdays**</u>

Main Idea: Birthdays are fun.

Details: 1. _____
2. _____
3. _____
4. _____

Retell Main Idea: I wish my birthday came more often.

2. Use these sentences to write a paragraph. Write the main idea, add the details, then retell the main idea. Indent the first sentence. Use capitals and periods. Remember to give the paragraph a title.

_____

_____

_____
_____
_____
_____
_____
_____
_____

© 1996 Kelley Wingate Publications   47   CD-3718

A paragraph contains a main idea and supporting details.

Every paragraph has one main idea. The main idea is called the **topic sentence**. It is usually the first sentence in the paragraph. The other sentences are **details** that tell more about the main idea. The last sentence retells the main idea.

1. Read the title and main idea of the paragraph. Write your own details.

Title of paragraph: <u>My Favorite Lunch</u>

Main Idea: Hamburgers and french fries are my favorite lunch.

Details: 1. _____
                      2. _____
                      3. _____
                      4. _____

Retell Main Idea: I would chose them for lunch any day!

2. Use these sentences to write a paragraph. Write the main idea, add the details, then retell the main idea. Indent the first sentence. Use capitals and periods. Remember to give the paragraph a title.

_____

_____

_____

_____

_____

_____

_____

_____

_____

_____

Name _____

| A paragraph contains a main idea and supporting details. |

Every paragraph has one main idea. The main idea is called the **topic sentence**. It is usually the first sentence in the paragraph. The other sentences are **details** that tell more about the main idea. The last sentence retells the main idea.

1. Choose an idea for your paragraph. Write the title, main idea, and details. Retell the main idea at the end.

Title of paragraph: _____

Main Idea: _____

Details: 1. _____

2. _____

3. _____

4. _____

Retell Main Idea: _____

2. Use these sentences to write a paragraph. Write the main idea, add the details, then retell the main idea. Indent the first sentence. Use capitals and periods. Remember to give the paragraph a title.

_____

_____

_____

_____

_____

_____

_____

A paragraph contains a main idea and supporting details.

Some paragraphs are written to persuade, or change the way people think. These paragraphs have a main idea and supporting details.

---

1. You must convince your mom to let you walk to the store to buy an apple. Give your reasons. Then ask again.

Title :   <u>Apple</u>

Question: May I walk to the store and buy an apple?

Reasons: 1. I will be careful crossing the street.
                   2. I have my own money to buy the apple.
                   3. It is early, so I will still be hungry for dinner.
                   4. I will help you set the table when I get back.

Ask again: Is it all right for me to go to the store?

---

2. Use these sentences to write a paragraph. Write the main ideas, add the details, then retell the main idea. Indent the first sentence. Use capitals and periods. Remember to give the paragraph a title.

_____

_____

_____

_____

_____

_____

_____

_____

_____

_____

A paragraph contains a main idea and supporting details.

Some paragraphs are written to persuade, or change the way people think. These paragraphs have a main idea and supporting details.

---

1. You must convince your teacher to let you change your desk from the front to the back of the room. Give your reasons. Then ask again.

Title : <u>Changing Desks</u>

Question: May I move my desk to the back of the classroom?

Reasons:
1. I will work better in the back of the room.
2. No one will bother me in the back of the class.
3. It is quieter in the back of the room.
4. I am too tall to sit in the front.

Ask again: May I move to the back of the room?

---

2. Use these sentences to write a paragraph. Write the main idea, add the details, then retell the main idea. Indent the first sentence. Use capitals and periods. Remember to give the paragraph a title.

_____

_____

_____

_____

_____

_____

_____

_____

_____

_____

Name _____ Skill: Persuasive Paragraphs

A paragraph contains a main idea and supporting details.

Some paragraphs are written to persuade, or change the way people think. These paragraphs have a main idea and supporting details.

_____

1. You must convince your mom and dad to let you have a puppy. Give your reasons. Then ask again.

Title : _____

Question: May I   _____

Reasons: 1. _____
             2. _____
             3. _____
             4. _____

Ask again: _____
_____

2. Use these sentences to write a paragraph. Write the main idea, add the details, then retell the main idea. Indent the first sentence. Use capitals and periods. Remember to give the paragraph a title.

_____

_____

_____

_____

_____

_____

_____

_____

_____

A paragraph contains a main idea and supporting details.

Some paragraphs are written to persuade, or change the way people think.
These paragraphs have a main idea and supporting details.

1. **You must convince your mom to let you play in the rain.**
Give your reasons. Then ask again.

Title : _____

Question: May I   _____

Reasons: 1. _____
                          2. _____
                          3. _____
                          4. _____

Ask again: _____

2. **Use these sentences to write a paragraph. Write the main idea, add the
details, then retell the main idea. Indent the first sentence. Use capitals and
periods. Remember to give the paragraph a title.**

_____

_____

_____

_____

_____

_____

_____

_____

_____

A paragraph contains a main idea and supporting details.

Some paragraphs are written to persuade, or change the way people think. These paragraphs have a main idea and supporting details.

1. You must convince your mom to buy you a bike for your birthday. Give your reasons. Then ask again.

Title : _____

Question: May I   _____

Reasons: 1. _____
                2. _____
                3. _____
                4. _____

Ask again: _____

2. Use these sentences to write a paragraph. Write the main idea, add the details, then retell the main idea. Indent the first sentence. Use capitals and periods. Remember to give the paragraph a title.

_____

_____

_____

_____

_____

_____

_____

_____

_____

A paragraph contains a main idea and supporting details.

Some paragraphs are written to persuade, or change the way people think. These paragraphs have a main idea and supporting details.

1. **You must convince your mom to let you play at a friend's house. Give your reasons. Then ask again.**

Title : _____

Question: May I   _____

Reasons: 1. _____
2. _____
3. _____
4. _____

Ask again: _____

2. **Use these sentences to write a paragraph. Write the main idea, add the details, then retell the main idea. Indent the first sentence. Use capitals and periods. Remember to give the paragraph a title.**

_____

_____

_____

_____

_____

_____

_____

_____

An invitation includes all the important facts.

"You are invited!" You must know <u>why, who, when, and, where</u>.
An invitation gives you all this information.

1. Read the invitation and answer the questions.

Halloween Party!

Given by:	Tony Black
Time:	7:00 p.m.
Date:	October 31
Place:	420 Apple Street

<u>Why</u> has the invitation been sent?

_____

<u>Who</u> is giving the party?

_____

<u>When</u> will you go?

_____

<u>Where</u> will you go?

_____

2. Make a birthday invitation. List the important information. Write the information on the invitation.

<u>Why</u> will the invitation be sent?

_____

<u>Who</u> is giving the party?

_____

<u>When</u> is the party?

_____

<u>Where</u> is the party?

_____

You're Invited!

COME _____

Given by: _____

Time: _____

Date: _____

Place: _____

Name _____   Skill: Invitations

| An invitation includes all the important facts. |

"You are invited!" You must know <u>why, who, when, and where</u>.
An invitation gives you all this information.

1. Read the invitation and answer the questions.

★★★★★★★★★★★★★★★★★★

Grand Opening!

Given by: Bob's Toy Store

Time: 10:00 a.m.

Date: June 14

Place: 856 Main Street

<u>Why</u> has the invitation been sent?

_____

<u>Who</u> is having the grand opening?

_____

<u>When</u> will you go?

_____

<u>Where</u> will you go?

_____

2. Write an invitation to a new park called Play Land. List the important information. Write the information on the invitation.

<u>Why</u> will the invitation be sent?

_____

<u>Who</u> is giving the party?

_____

<u>When</u> is the party?

_____

<u>Where</u> is the party?

_____

You're Invited!

COME _____

Given by: _____

Time: _____

Date: _____

Place: _____

© 1996 Kelley Wingate Publications   57   CD-3718

An invitation includes all the important facts.

"You are invited!" You must know <u>why, who, when, and where</u>.
An invitation gives you all this information.

1. **Read the invitation and answer the questions.**

Come to Our Class Play!
Given by: Mrs. Bar's 3rd Grade Class
Time: 2:00 p.m.
Date: December 15
Place: Martin Elementary School

<u>Why</u> has the invitation been sent?

_____

<u>Who</u> is giving the play?

_____

<u>When</u> will you go?

_____

<u>Where</u> will you go?

_____

2. **Write an invitation to a parent's meeting at school. List the important information. Write the information on the invitation.**

<u>Why</u> will the invitation be sent?

_____

<u>Who</u> is giving the party?

_____

<u>When</u> is the party?

_____

<u>Where</u> is the party?

_____

You're Invited!
COME _____
Given by: _____
Time: _____
Date: _____
Place: _____

An invitation includes all the important facts.

"You are invited!" You must know <u>why, who, when, and where</u>.
An invitation gives you all this information.

1. Read the invitation and answer the questions.

Pet Show!

Given by: The City Pet Shelter

Time: 9:00 a.m.

Date: May 9

Place: 127 Kitten Street

<u>Why</u> has the invitation been sent?

_____

<u>Who</u> is giving the show?

_____

<u>When</u> will you go?

_____

<u>Where</u> will you go?

_____

_____

**2. Write an invitation to a school fair. List the important information.
Write the information on the invitation.**

<u>Why</u> will the invitation be sent?

_____

<u>Who</u> is giving the party?

_____

<u>When</u> is the party?

_____

<u>Where</u> is the party?

_____

You're Invited!

COME _____

Given by: _____

Time: _____

Date: _____

Place: _____

Name _____   Skill: Invitations

| An invitation includes all the important facts. |

"You are invited!" You must know <u>why, who, when, and where</u>.
An invitation gives you all this information.

1. Read the invitation and answer the questions.

Dinner Party!

Given by: Anne Winters

Time: 7:00 p.m.

Date: November 27

Place: 608 Lake Drive

<u>Why</u> has the invitation been sent?

_____

<u>Who</u> is giving the party?

_____

<u>When</u> will you go?

_____

<u>Where</u> will you go?

_____

**2. Write an invitation to a skating party. List the important information.
Write the information on the invitation.**

<u>Why</u> will the invitation be sent?

_____

<u>Who</u> is giving the party?

_____

<u>When</u> is the party?

_____

<u>Where</u> is the party?

_____

You're Invited!

COME _____

Given by: _____

Time: _____

Date: _____

Place: _____

| An invitation includes all the important facts. |

"You are invited!" You must know <u>why, who, when, and where</u>.
An invitation gives you all this information.

1. Make your own invitation and illustrate it. Answer the questions.

_____

Given by: _____

Time: _____

Date: _____

Place: _____

<u>Why</u> has the invitation been sent?

_____

<u>Who</u> is giving the party?

_____

<u>When</u> will you go?

_____

<u>Where</u> will you go?

_____

2. Make your own invitation. List the important information. Write the information on the invitation.

<u>Why</u> will the invitation be sent?

_____

<u>Who</u> is giving the party?

_____

<u>When</u> is the party?

_____

<u>Where</u> is the party?

_____

You're Invited!

_____

Given by: _____

Time: _____

Date: _____

Place: _____

A friendly letter has 5 parts: date, greeting, body, closing, and signature.

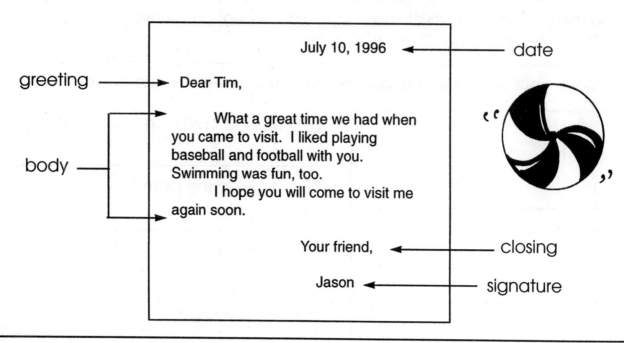

greeting

body

July 10, 1996 ← date

Dear Tim,

What a great time we had when you came to visit. I liked playing baseball and football with you. Swimming was fun, too.
I hope you will come to visit me again soon.

Your friend, ← closing

Jason ← signature

Write a letter to your friend. Talk about things you like to do together.

_____
(date)

_____
(greeting)

_____

_____

_____ (body)

_____

_____

_____
(closing)

_____
(signature)

A friendly letter has 5 parts: date, greeting, body, closing, and signature.

1. Read these letter parts. Rewrite each part in the proper place on the letter form at the right.

_____

Dear Aunt Carol,

Amanda

February 3

Love,

    Thank you for the new red shirt you sent for my birthday. I really love it. I will wear it to school on Monday.

_____ (date)

_____ (greeting)

_____
_____
_____
_____
_____
_____

_____ (closing)

_____ (signature)

2. Write a letter to your grandmother. Thank her for the gift she sent you. Be sure to put a comma after the greeting and closing.

A friendly letter has 5 parts: date, greeting, body, closing, and signature.

1. Write a letter to your teacher. Thank her for taking you on a field trip.
Include all 5 parts of a letter. Be sure to put a comma after the greeting and
closing.

2. Write a letter to your classmate. Ask him to come to your house on
Saturday. Write about the things you will do when he comes.

Name _____

> A friendly letter has 5 parts: date, greeting, body, closing, and signature.

Write a letter to your new friend.

Describe yourself.

Tell what you like to do.

Describe your room.

Describe your family.

A friendly letter has 5 parts: date, greeting, body, closing, and signature.

1. **Write a letter to a firefighter. What would you like to ask her?**

1. _____

2. _____

3. _____

4. _____

5. _____

2. **Use the above questions to write your letter.**

| A friendly letter has 5 parts: date, greeting, body, closing, and signature. |

Write a letter to someone you know.

_____

_____

_____

_____

_____

_____

_____

_____

_____

_____

_____

_____

_____

_____

_____

_____

_____

_____

It is important to address an envelope correctly. An envelope shows who is sending a letter and who is receiving a letter. Name, address, city, state, and zip code must be placed in the proper places.

The sender is : A	**The receiver is** : D
His house address is : B	**His house address is** : E
His city, state, and zip code are : C	**His city, state, and zip code are** : F

1. Study the completed envelope.

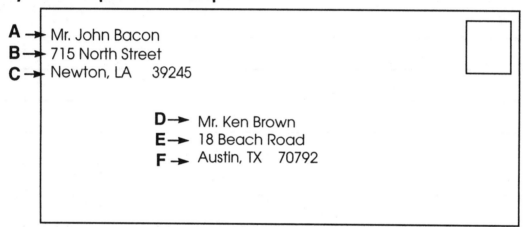

A → Mr. John Bacon
B → 715 North Street
C → Newton, LA   39245

D → Mr. Ken Brown
E → 18 Beach Road
F → Austin, TX   70792

2. Address the envelope below with the information given.

The sender is:
   Miss Karen Taylor
   562 Clover Road
   Jackson, MS   44823

The receiver is:
   Mrs. Donna Burns
   74 Valley Street
   Buffalo, NY 48704

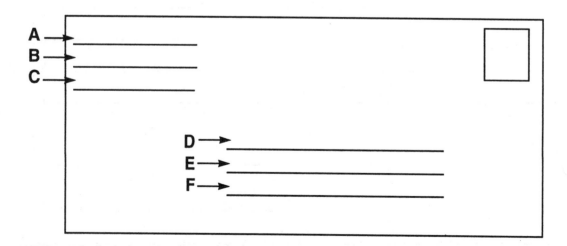

It is important to address an envelope correctly. An envelope shows who is sending a letter and who is receiving a letter. Name, address, city, state, and zip code must be placed in the proper places.

1. Address the envelope below with the information given.

The sender is:
> Dr. James Madison
> 38 Carlton Place
> Salem, NC   89532

The receiver is:
> Ms. Mary Morton
> 149 Sparrow Street
> Tucson, AZ   52974

2. Address the envelope below with the information given.

The sender is:
> Mrs. Alice Wilson
> 9 Flag Avenue
> Port Huron, MI   48060

The receiver is:
> Miss Susan Coats
> 183 Spring Street
> Denver, CO   50738

It is important to address an envelope correctly. An envelope shows who is sending a letter and who is receiving a letter. Name, address, city, state, and zip code must be placed in the proper places.

1. Address the envelope below with the information given.

The sender is:
Mr. Martin Guy
77 Troy Avenue
Toronto, Ontario   M9L 1Z1

The receiver is:
Mrs. Cindy Lesson
293 Park Place
Conner, RI   24375

2. Address the envelope below with the information given.

The sender is:
Ms. Lynn Sprat
14 Woods Drive
Miami, FL   66931

The receiver is:
Miss Lisa Kent
941 York Street
Madison, WI   22814

It is important to address an envelope correctly. An envelope shows who is sending a letter and who is receiving a letter. Name, address, city, state, and zip code must be placed in the proper places.

1. Address the envelope below with the information given.

The sender is:
   Dr. Joe Scott
   253 Forest Lane
   Atlanta, GA   34274

The receiver is:
   Mr. Alan Smith
   174 Star Road
   Salem, OR   69274

2. Address the envelope below with the information given.

The sender is:
   Mr. Don Davis
   33 Leland Place
   Wheeling, PA   81475

The receiver is:
   Mrs. Sharon Keys
   590 Broad Street
   Tulsa, OK   42851

It is important to address an envelope correctly. An envelope shows who is sending a letter and who is receiving a letter. Name, address, city, state, and zip code must be placed in the proper places.

1. Address this envelope to someone you know.

2. Address this envelope to someone you know.

Name _____   Skill: Descriptive Writing

| Adjectives are words that describe which, how many, what color, and what an object looks or feels like. |

Adjectives make stories more colorful and interesting.
They help you "see" a story in your imagination.

For each picture below list 4 adjectives to describe it. Write a paragraph about each picture. Use your adjectives. Write a title for your paragraph.

1. _____   2. _____

3. _____   4. _____

_____

_____

_____

_____

_____

_____

_____

1. _____   2. _____

3. _____   4. _____

_____

_____

_____

_____

_____

_____

> **Adjectives are words that describe which, how many, what color, and what an object looks or feels like.**

Adjectives make stories more colorful and interesting.
They help you "see" a story in your imagination.

For each picture below list 4 adjectives to describe it. Write a paragraph about each picture. Use your adjectives. Write a title for your paragraph.

1. _____ 2. _____

3. _____ 4. _____

_____

_____

_____

_____

_____

_____

_____

_____

1. _____ 2. _____

3. _____ 4. _____

_____

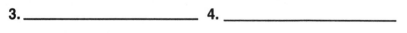

_____

_____

_____

_____

_____

> **Adjectives are words that describe which, how many, what color, and what an object looks or feels like.**

Adjectives make stories more colorful and interesting.
They help you "see" a story in your imagination.

1. Read the following paragraph.

I have a favorite pair of shoes. They are old. My mom doesn't like them. She wants me to throw them away and get a new pair. I would rather keep my old shoes.

2. Now, read the same paragraph with adjectives and more description added.

I have a favorite pair of shoes. They are old and comfortable. The shoes are blue and white. The left shoe has a hole in the toe, and the right has a broken shoelace. Both of them have holes worn in the bottom. My mom doesn't like my old shoes. They are very dirty. She wants me to throw them away and get a new pair. I would rather keep my old, comfy, worn out shoes.

3. Read the following paragraph then make it more interesting. Use adjectives to rewrite it.

Yesterday my family took a train ride. There was an engine, passenger cars, and box cars. A caboose was at the end. The whistle blew. We were off! Smoke blew from the engine. The cars began to rock. I would like to ride on a train again.

_____

_____

_____

_____

_____

_____

_____

_____

_____

_____

> **Adjectives are words that describe which, how many, what color, and what an object looks or feels like.**

Adjectives make stories more colorful and interesting.
They help you "see" a story in your imagination.

1. Read the following paragraph.

I like to watch the sunset. The colors are beautiful. Sometimes the sun peeks through the clouds and makes more colors. As the sun sinks, the sky becomes darker. Soon night will be here and stars will come out.

2. Now, read the same paragraph with adjectives and more description added.

I like to watch the sunset. The red and orange colors are beautiful. Sometimes the sun peeks between clouds, turning them pink and purple. As the sun sinks, the evening sky becomes a dark blue then black. Soon the inky night sky will shine with bright stars.

3. Read the following paragraph then make it more interesting. Use adjectives to rewrite it.

My sister and I went for a walk in the forest. We came to a gingerbread house. I thought it looked very strange. My sister thought it looked tasty. We will never forget that house in the woods.

_____

_____

_____

_____

_____

_____

_____

_____

_____

> **Adjectives are words that describe which, how many, what color, and what an object looks or feels like.**

Adjectives make stories more colorful and interesting.
They help you "see" a story in your imagination.

1. Read this paragraph.

I live in a house. It is built out of bricks. There is a fence around the yard. I planted flowers in the gardens. My house looks pretty.

2. This is the same paragraph with adjectives and more description added.

I live in a small, neat house. It is built out of brown and white bricks. There is a tall, wooden fence around the large yard. I planted beautiful red and yellow flowers in the front and back gardens. My little house looks pretty.

3. Read this paragraph then make it more interesting. Use adjectives to rewrite it.

Winter is here. All the trees are bare. It is cold outside. Children are wearing warm clothes. Smoke rises from chimneys. Soon it will be snowing. Everything will be covered in snow. It is time for plants and some animals to go to sleep for the winter. Winter is a nice season.

_____

_____

_____

_____

_____

_____

_____

_____

_____

_____

Name _____ Skill: Compare and Contrast

Some things can be both alike and different.

1. Fill in the blanks with words that tell how a tree and flower are alike and different. The first one has been done for you.

tree   flower

different   **alike**   **different**

1. _____Trunk_____   1. _____Roots_____   1. _____Stem_____

2. _____   2. _____   2. _____

3. _____   3. _____   3. _____

2. Write two paragraphs below. In the first paragraph tell how trees and flowers are alike. Tell how each is different in the second paragraph. Title your story.

_____

_____

_____

_____

_____

_____

_____

_____

_____

_____

_____

Some things can be both alike and different.

1. Fill in the blanks with words that tell how a cat and a dog are alike and different. The first one has been done for you.

<u>cat</u>   <u>dog</u>

different   **alike**   **different**

1. <u>pointed ears</u>   1. <u>furry</u>   1. <u>floppy ears</u>

2. _____   2. _____   2. _____

3. _____   3. _____   3. _____

2. Write two paragraphs below. In the first paragraph tell how cats and dogs are alike. Tell how each is different in the second paragraph. Title your story.

_____

_____

_____
_____
_____
_____
_____
_____
_____
_____
_____

Name _____

Some things can be both alike and different.

1. Fill in the blanks with words that tell how lettuce and carrots are alike and different. The first one has been done for you.

lettuce   carrots

different   **alike**   **different**

1. green _____   1. vegetables _____   1. orange _____

2. _____   2. _____   2. _____

3. _____   3. _____   3. _____

2. Write two paragraphs below. In the first paragraph tell how lettuce and carrots are alike. Tell how each is different in the second paragraph. Title your story.

_____

_____

_____

_____

_____

_____

_____

_____

_____

_____

_____

Some things can be both alike and different.

1. Fill in the blanks with words that tell how a watch and a clock are alike and different. The first one has been done for you.

<u>watch</u>   <u>clock</u>

different	alike	different
1. <u>has a wrist band</u>	1. <u>both have hands</u>	1. <u>has a base</u>
2. _____	2. _____	2. _____
3. _____	3. _____	3. _____

2. Write two paragraphs below. In the first paragraph tell how watches and clocks are alike. Tell how each is different in the second paragraph. Title your story.

_____

_____

_____

_____

_____

_____

_____

_____

_____

_____

_____

Some things can be both alike and different.

1. Fill in the lines with words that tell how corn and a banana are alike and different.

banana   **corn**

different   alike   different

1. _____   1. _____   1. _____

2. _____   2. _____   2. _____

3. _____   3. _____   3. _____

2. Write two paragraphs below. In the first paragraph tell how bananas and corn are alike. Tell how each is different in the second paragraph. Title your story.

_____

_____

_____

_____

_____

_____

_____

_____

_____

_____

_____

A sentence ends in a punctuation mark.

1. Place the correct punctuation mark at the end of each sentence.
Add an ending to the story.

Digging For Worms

Once upon a time there was a boy named Jake   Jake and his mother
were very poor and hungry   One day Jake was digging for worms to eat
He dug and dug   Soon he was in a deep hole   It was so deep that he could
not climb out   Suddenly a giant worm stuck his head out of the dirt at the
bottom of the hole   Jake was frightened   He looked at the worm and

_____

_____

_____

_____

_____

2. Write your own story about giant worms. Use correct punctuation.

_____

_____

_____

_____

_____

_____

_____

| A sentence ends in a punctuation mark. |

**1. Place the correct punctuation mark at the end of each sentence.
Add an ending to the story.**

Backwards-Inside-Out Day

Today is a "Backwards-Inside-Out-Day" at school   Everyone must come to school with their clothes on backwards and inside-out   Shirts and pants must be worn backwards   Sweaters and belts should be on backwards   Everything is turned inside-out   Some things cannot be worn backwards or inside-out   You can't wear your shoes backwards   What do we do then   We wear things that don't match   I will wear one black shoe and one red shoe   I think my teacher

_____

_____

_____

_____

_____

_____

**2. What would you wear on "Backward-Inside-Out" day?
Use correct punctuation.**

_____

_____

_____

_____

_____

_____

_____

_____

| A sentence ends in a punctuation mark. |

1. Place the correct punctuation mark at the end of each sentence. Add an ending to the story.

Making Pancakes

My sister and I woke up early last Saturday morning   We decided to make breakfast for Mom   We took out the pancake mix   We put the mix in a big bowl   We added eggs and milk   I was stirring the batter   My sister was pouring orange juice   Just then the cat jumped up onto the counter   He tipped over the glass of juice and knocked the bowl to the floor   Batter and juice were everywhere   Just then

_____

_____

_____

_____

_____

_____

2. Write about something you have cooked. Use correct punctuation.

_____

_____

_____

_____

_____

_____

_____

_____

Sentences and proper nouns begin with capital letters.

Place capital letters where they are needed. Add an ending to the story.

a stormy night

it was a stormy, dark, october night. robin and i were frightened. the wind was whistling through the trees. lightening flashes danced off the windows. thunder was rumbling across the sky. we were all alone in the house. mom and dad had gone to aunt jan's home for a dinner party. we hoped that they would be back soon. we always stayed up late on saturday nights, but tonight we were already under the covers. our dog, taffy, was in bed with us. she was afraid, too. just then we heard a knock at the door. "who is it?" i called. we looked out the window and there stood

_____

_____

_____

_____

_____

_____

_____

_____

_____

_____

_____

Sentences and proper nouns begin with capital letters.

Place capital letters where they are needed. Add an ending to the story.

my birthday

today is my birthday. i am nine years old. i was born on wednesday, april

12 in billings, montana. my family will celebrate my birthday tonight. mom will

cook her special spaghetti dinner just for me. dad will be home from work

early. my brother, david, and my sister, rose, will be here, too. after dinner

grandma and grandpa will come. we will all eat cake and ice cream. they

will sing "happy birthday" to me. then i

_____

_____

_____

_____

_____

_____

_____

_____

_____

_____

_____

_____

_____

Sentences and proper nouns begin with capital letters.

Place capital letters where they are needed. Add an ending to the story.

the magic show

aunt gail took me to a magic show last thursday afternoon. the show was held at the adams theater on river road. the magician's name was morton the magnificent. morton was wonderful! he made two birds disappear. he made a quarter appear from behind frank hopkin's ear. morton made a flower out of paper. when he waved a wand over it, the flower became real. he asked mr. rogers to come up on stage. morton made mr. rogers float through the air. morton chose aunt gail for another trick. he put her into a long box so only her head and feet showed. he took a saw and began to cut the box in half. aunt gail screamed and i

_____

_____

_____

_____

_____

_____

_____

_____

_____

Sentences need punctuation marks.
Sentences and proper nouns begin with capital letters.

**Place punctuation marks and capital letters where they are needed.
Add an ending to the story.**

the adventure of baby bird

mother bird was busy with her three new babies they were growing so

quickly soon they would all begin flying they were always hungry she could

never seem to find enough food to keep them full back and forth she flew all

day long with worms and bugs

chirpy was the smallest of the three babies he was also the bravest he

liked to jump to the edge of the nest to see his new world mother bird warned

him to be careful she said that he might fall from the nest there were cats in

the yard below how would he get home if he fell out of the nest

mother bird flew away to get the babies their dinner chirpy hopped right

up on the edge of the nest suddenly his foot slipped he began to fall

_____

_____

_____

_____

_____

_____

_____

_____

> **Sentences need punctuation marks.**
> **Sentences and proper nouns begin with capital letters.**

Place punctuation marks and capital letters where they are needed.
Add an ending to the story.

be careful what you wish for

robert heard someone calling his name   he looked all around   he could not see anyone   he was all alone on the sidewalk   all of his friends had gone inside to start their homework or have dinner   he heard someone call him again   who could it be   he listened carefully   the voice seemed to be coming from inside his bookbag   robert opened his bookbag and looked inside   there stood a tiny man dressed in a green suit   he was wearing red shoes and a hat with bells on it

the tiny man said his name was elvin   he was a magic elf   he told robert to wish for whatever he wanted   elvin said he would make the wish come true   robert thought about ice cream   zap   there was an ice cream cone in his hand   robert began to grin   this was going to be great   robert decided

_____

_____

_____

_____

_____

_____

Sentences need punctuation marks.
Sentences and proper nouns begin with capital letters.

Place punctuation marks and capital letters where they are needed.
Add an ending to the story.

tell the truth

my little sister penny had a hard time telling the truth   she made up stories

all the time   she was always getting herself in trouble   sometimes she made

me a part of her stories   and i got in trouble too   my mother told her to stop

making up stories   mother said that penny's nose would start to grow every

time she told a lie   penny would look just like pinnochio   penny just laughed

she did not believe mom

one day penny ran into the house   she said that a dinosaur was coming

down our street   penny's nose began to twitch   it

_____

_____

_____

_____

_____

_____

_____

_____

_____

_____

| Proofread work to correct punctuation, capitals, and spelling. |

The first copy of a story is called a "rough draft".   When you read your "rough draft" you may find mistakes. Correct any mistakes then rewrite your "rough draft" as a final copy.

Example: Gary and ~~i went~~ **I went** to the store last ~~monday~~ **Monday**. We ~~bot~~ **bought** candy **.**

1. Use these lines to write a "rough draft". Proofread your story and correct it.

_____

_____

_____

_____

_____

_____

_____

_____

2. Use the corrected "rough draft" to write your final copy below.

_____

_____

_____

_____

_____

_____

_____

_____

Name_____

| Actions tell us about characters. |

Characters tell us about themselves by the way they act. These actions make something happen in a story. When we understand characters and their actions, we understand the story.

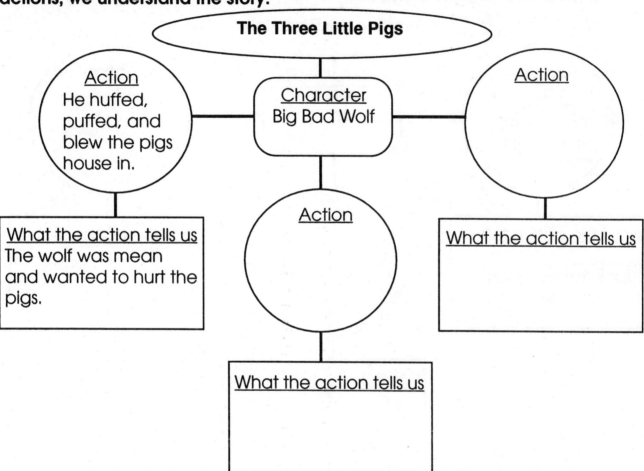

1. **Complete the chart. Use the information to write about the Big Bad Wolf.**

_____

_____

_____

_____

_____

_____

_____

                                       CD-3718

Name_____ Skill: Character Webs

| Actions tell us about characters. |

Characters tell us about themselves by the way they act. These actions make something happen in a story. When we understand characters and their actions, we understand the story.

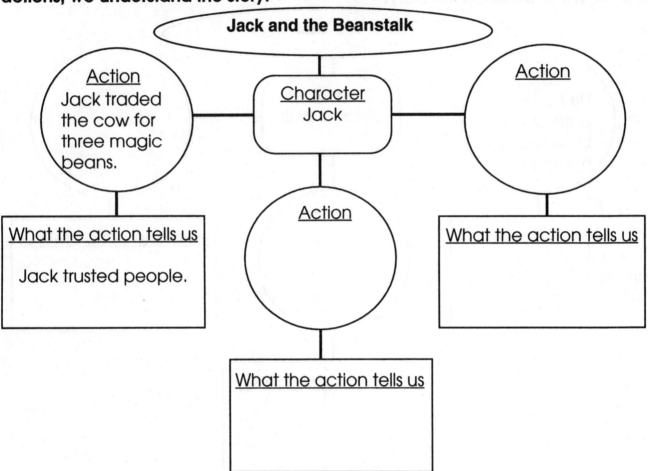

Jack and the Beanstalk

Action
Jack traded the cow for three magic beans.

Character
Jack

Action

Action

What the action tells us

Jack trusted people.

What the action tells us

What the action tells us

Complete the chart. Use the information to write about Jack.

_____

_____

_____

_____

_____

_____

_____

94

Actions tell us about characters.

Characters tell us about themselves by the way they act. These actions make something happen in a story. When we understand characters and their actions, we understand the story.

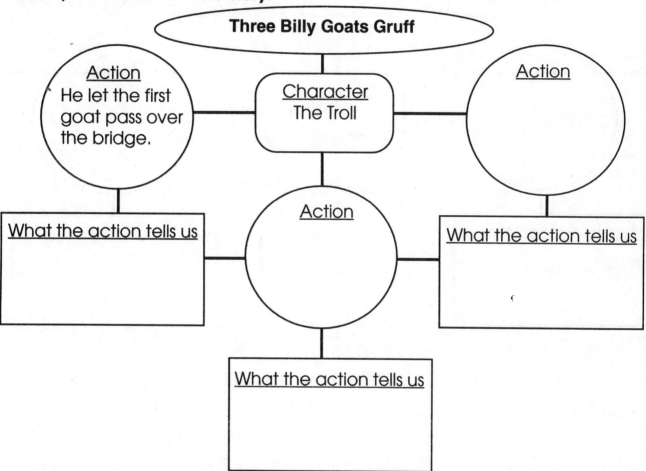

Complete the chart. Use the information to write about the Troll.

_____

_____

_____

_____

_____

_____

Actions tell us about characters.

Characters tell us about themselves by the way they act. These actions make something happen in a story. When we understand characters and their actions, we understand the story.

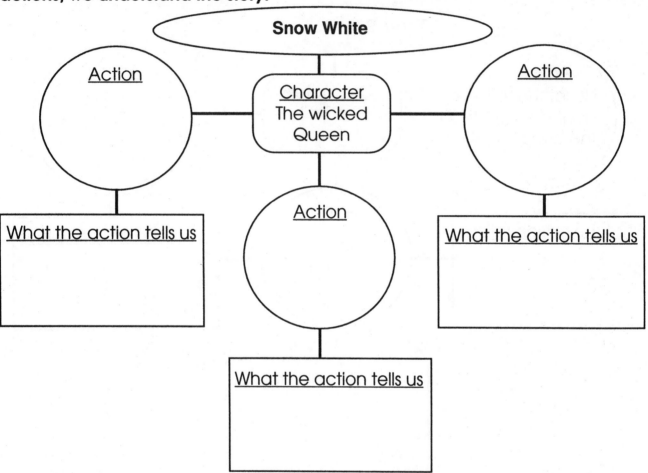

Complete the chart. Use the information to write about the wicked Queen.

_____

_____

_____

_____

_____

_____

Actions tell us about characters.

Characters tell us about themselves by the way they act. These actions make something happen in a story. When we understand characters and their actions, we understand the story.

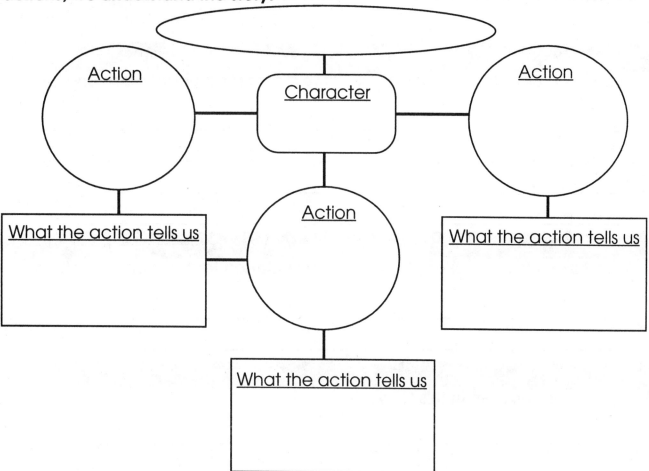

Complete the chart. Use the information to write your story.

_____

_____

_____

_____

_____

_____

_____

Book Report

Title:

Author:

1. **Name two characters in this book. Write a sentence about each one.**

1. _____   _____

   _____   _____

2. _____   _____

   _____   _____

2. **Tell where this story takes place. Write a sentence to describe the setting.**

_____

_____

3. **What is the problem in this story?**

_____

_____

_____

_____

4. **How is the problem solved?**

_____

_____

_____

_____

About This Book

Characters
_____
_____
_____

_____ (title)

By: _____ (author)

(end)

(middle)

(beginning)

CD-3718

Book Review

Title: _____

Author: _____

1. Retell the story in your own words. Be sure to include the characters, setting, beginning, middle, and end.

_____

_____

_____

_____

_____

_____

_____

_____

_____

_____

2. What did you like most about this book? Tell why and use examples from the book.

_____

_____

_____

_____

_____

_____

_____

_____

_____

Writing Award

_____

receives this award for

_____

Keep up the great work!

_____ _____
signed   date

Writing Whiz!

_____

receives this award for

_____

Great Job!

_____ _____
signed   date

                                       CD-3718

Wonderful Writing!

_____

receives this award for

_____

Keep up the great work!

_____

signed   date

All Star Writer

_____

is a Writing All Star!

_____

You are terrific!

_____

signed   date

CD-3718

Answer Key

Name _____ Skill: Creative Writing

September

Write a story about things you do during September.

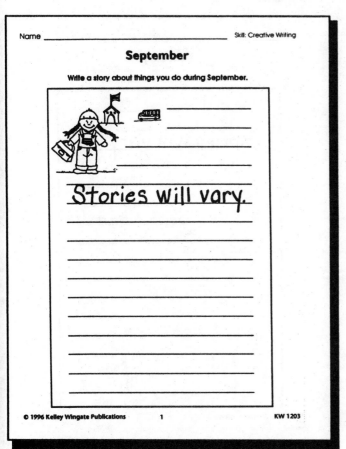

Stories will vary.

© 1996 Kelley Wingate Publications   1   KW 1203

Name _____ Skill: Creative Writing

October

Write a story about things you do during October.

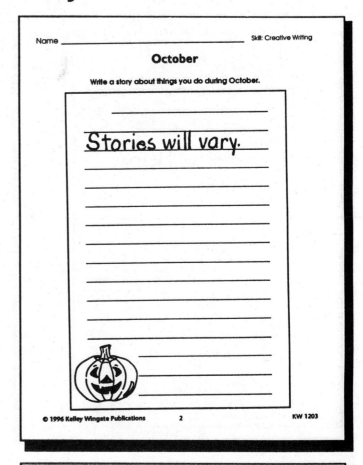

Stories will vary.

© 1996 Kelley Wingate Publications   2   KW 1203

Name _____ Skill: Creative Writing

November

Write a story about things you do during November.

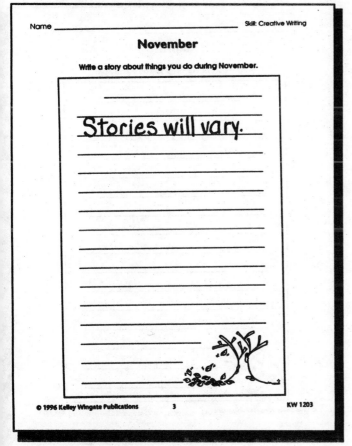

Stories will vary.

© 1996 Kelley Wingate Publications   3   KW 1203

Name _____ Skill: Creative Writing

December

Write a story about things you do during December.

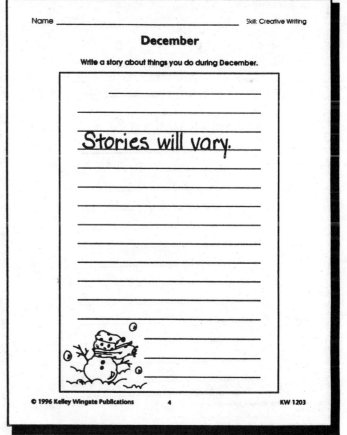

Stories will vary.

© 1996 Kelley Wingate Publications   4   KW 1203

Answer Key

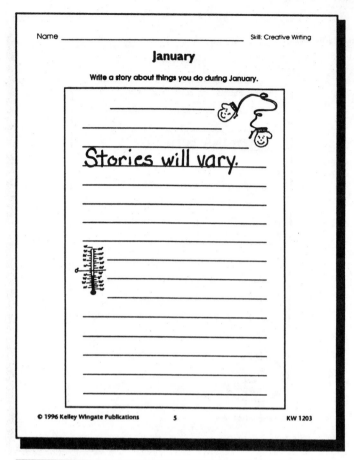

Name _____

Skill: Creative Writing

January

Write a story about things you do during January.

Stories will vary.

5 KW 1203

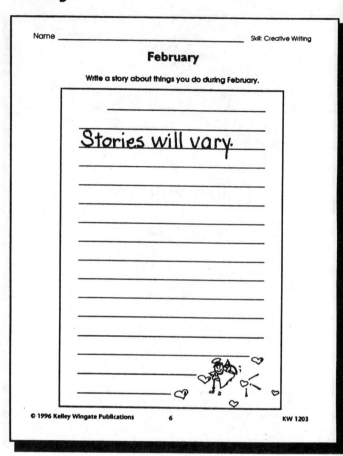

Name _____

Skill: Creative Writing

February

Write a story about things you do during February.

Stories will vary.

6 KW 1203

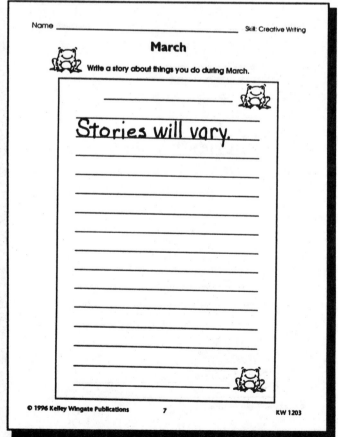

Name _____

Skill: Creative Writing

March

Write a story about things you do during March.

Stories will vary.

7 KW 1203

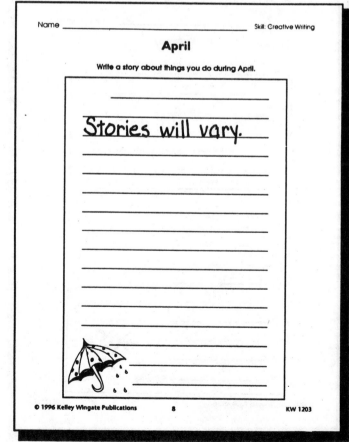

Name _____

Skill: Creative Writing

April

Write a story about things you do during April.

Stories will vary.

8 KW 1203

Answer Key

Name _____   Skill: Creative Writing

May

Write a story about things you do during May.

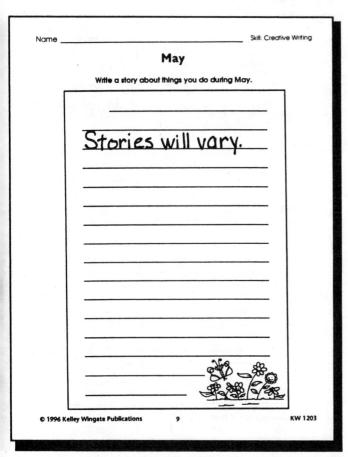

Stories will vary.

Name _____   Skill: Creative Writing

June

Write a story about things you do during June.

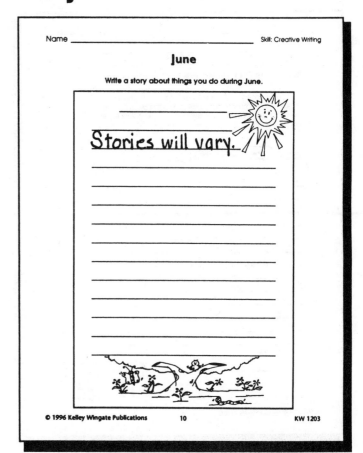

Stories will vary.

Name _____   Skill: Creative Writing

July

Write a story about things you do during July.

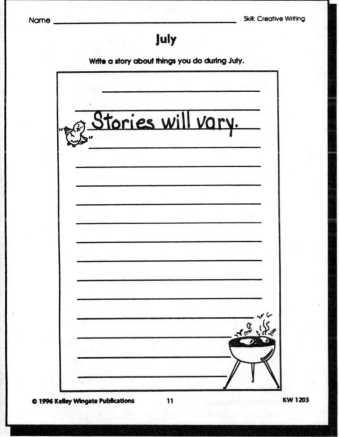

Stories will vary.

Name _____   Skill: Creative Writing

August

Write a story about things you do during August.

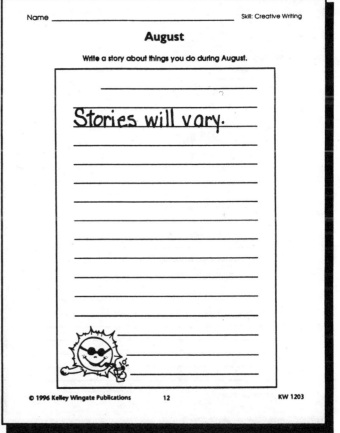

Stories will vary.

Answer Key

Name _____ Skill: Story Completion

Stories have a beginning, a middle, and an end.

Finish this story. Add a middle and an end. Be sure to use capitals and periods.

Susan sat down in her desk at school. She started to put her books away. A new student walked into the classroom. She sat in the desk next to Susan. The new student looked very frightened. Susan

Stories will vary.

13 KW 1203

Name _____ Skill: Story Completion

Stories have a beginning, a middle, and an end.

Finish this story. Add a middle and an end. Be sure to use capitals and periods.

"Happy birthday!" said Eric's mom and dad. "We have decided that you may have a pet as your birthday present. Let's go to the pet store."
"Great!" said Eric. "I know just the pet I would like to have."

Stories will vary.

14 KW 1203

Name _____ Skill: Story Completion

Stories have a beginning, a middle, and an end.

Finish this story. Add a middle and an end. Be sure to use capitals and periods.

Jim loves to swim. He and his friends go swimming in the lake every day. Everyone agrees that Jim and Ron are the best swimmers. One day Jim and Ron decided to have a race across the lake. They stood on the dock and dove in at the same time.

Stories will vary.

15 KW 1203

Name _____ Skill: Story Completion

Stories have a beginning, a middle, and an end.

Finish this story. Add a middle and an end. Be sure to use capitals and periods.

Pam's dog Mason loved to chase cats. One morning when they were out for a walk a big white cat raced across their path. Mason barked at the cat. Pam could feel him pull on his leash. "No, Mason! Stop!" cried Pam, but it was too late.

Stories will vary.

16 KW 1203

 CD-3718

Answer Key

Stories have a beginning, a middle, and an end.

Name _____ Skill: Story Completion

Stories have a beginning, a middle, and an end.

Finish this story. Add a middle and an end. Be sure to use capitals and periods.

The weatherman said that a terrible storm would be coming to our city. Dark clouds began to turn the sky black. Thunder boomed and lightening flashed. Rain began to pour on the roof. There was a streak of lightening and the lights went out. Our house was in total darkness.

Stories will vary.

© 1996 Kelley Wingate Publications   17   KW 1203

Name _____ Skill: Word Box Stories

Stories have a beginning, a middle, and an end.

Write five more words about the picture in the word box. Use the words to write a story. Be sure to use capitals and periods. Think of a title for your story.

Things To Think About
Who is this story about? Where does this story take place? How does this story begin? What happens next? How will you make this story end?

Word Box

children	bus
noisy	laugh
yellow	shiny
school	jump

(Words will vary)

School Bus

I am a shiny yellow bus. I pick up children and take them to school. The boys and girls love to ride in me. They jump up my steps and bounce on my seats. I am almost sad at the end of my trip when my doors open and the children leave me for the day.

© 1996 Kelley Wingate Publications   18   KW 1203

Name _____ Skill: Word Box Stories

Stories have a beginning, a middle, and an end.

Write five more words about the picture in the word box. Use the words to write a story. Be sure to use capitals and periods. Think of a title for your story.

Things To Think About
Who is this story about? Where does this story take place? How does this story begin? What happens next? How will you make this story end?

Word Box

trick-or-treat	face
pumpkin	orange
scary	green
carve	knife

(Words will vary)

Stories will vary.

© 1996 Kelley Wingate Publications   19   KW 1203

Name _____ Skill: Word Box Stories

Stories have a beginning, a middle, and an end.

Write five more words about the picture in the word box. Use the words to write a story. Be sure to use capitals and periods. Think of a title for your story.

Things To Think About
Who is this story about? Where does this story take place? How does this story begin? What happens next? How will you make this story end?

Word Box

Eskimo	warm
snow	coat
ice hole	gloves
fishing	hat

(Words will vary)

Stories will vary.

© 1996 Kelley Wingate Publications   20   KW 1203

Answer Key

Name _____   Skill: Word Box Stories

Stories have a beginning, a middle, and an end.

Write five more words about the picture in the word box. Use the words to write a story. Be sure to use capitals and periods. Think of a title for your story.

— Things To Think About —
Who is this story about? Where does this story take place? How does this story begin? What happens next? How will you make this story end?

Word Box

bird   egg
crack   yellow
spring   fluffy
Chick   cute

(words will vary)

Stories will vary.

© 1996 Kelley Wingate Publications   21   KW 1203

Name _____   Skill: Word Box Stories

Stories have a beginning, a middle, and an end.

Write five more words about the picture in the word box. Use the words to write a story. Be sure to use capitals and periods. Think of a title for your story.

— Things To Think About —
Who is this story about? Where does this story take place? How does this story begin? What happens next? How will you make this story end?

Word Box

crunchy   chips
warm   cookies
beverage   milk
chocolate   tasty

(words will vary)

Stories will vary.

© 1996 Kelley Wingate Publications   22   KW 1203

Name _____   Skill: Word Box Stories

Stories have a beginning, a middle, and an end.

Write five more words about the picture in the word box. Use the words to write a story. Be sure to use capitals and periods. Think of a title for your story.

— Things To Think About —
Who is this story about? Where does this story take place? How does this story begin? What happens next? How will you make this story end?

Word Box

ocean   colorful
treasure chest   swim
blue   shells
fish   green

(words will vary)

Stories will vary.

© 1996 Kelley Wingate Publications   23   KW 1203

Name _____   Skill: Word Box Stories

Stories have a beginning, a middle, and an end.

Write five more words about the picture in the word box. Use the words to write a story. Be sure to use capitals and periods. Think of a title for your story.

— Things To Think About —
Who is this story about? Where does this story take place? How does this story begin? What happens next? How will you make this story end?

Word Box

autumn   falling
orange   crunch
yellow   crisp
leaf   cool

(words will vary)

Stories will vary.

© 1996 Kelley Wingate Publications   24   KW 1203

Answer Key

Page 25

Name _____   Skill: Story Web

| Stories have a beginning, a middle, and an end. |

Finish the story web. Use the words in the web to write a story about
the picture. Be sure to use capitals and periods. Think of a title for your story.

Things To Think About
Who is this story about? Where does this story take place? How does
this story begin? What happens next? How will you make this story end?

bread   basket
blanket   Picnic   **ants**
chicken   **apples**

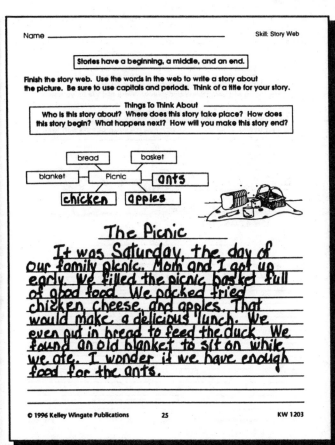

The Picnic
It was Saturday, the day of
our family picnic. Mom and I got up
early. We filled the picnic basket full
of good food. We packed fried
chicken, cheese, and apples. That
would make a delicious lunch. We
even put in bread to feed the duck. We
found an old blanket to sit on while
we ate. I wonder if we have enough
food for the ants.

© 1996 Kelley Wingate Publications   25   KW 1203

Page 26

Name _____   Skill: Story Web

| Stories have a beginning, a middle, and an end. |

Finish the story web. Use the words in the web to write a story about
the picture. Be sure to use capitals and periods. Think of a title for your story.

Things To Think About
Who is this story about? Where does this story take place? How does
this story begin? What happens next? How will you make this story end?

cactus   hot
camel   desert   **wind**
sand   **sunset**
(Words will vary)

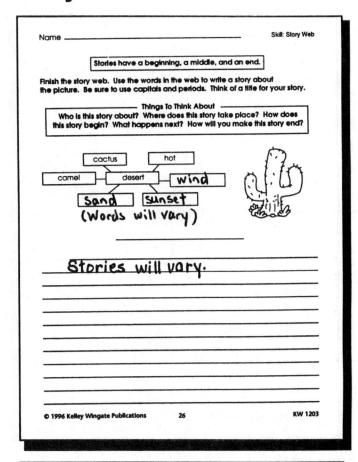

Stories will vary.

© 1996 Kelley Wingate Publications   26   KW 1203

Page 27

Name _____   Skill: Story Web

| Stories have a beginning, a middle, and an end. |

Finish the story web. Use the words in the web to write a story about
the picture. Be sure to use capitals and periods. Think of a title for your story.

Things To Think About
Who is this story about? Where does this story take place? How does
this story begin? What happens next? How will you make this story end?

scarf   skis
snow   Skiing   **down**
hill   **pole**
(Words will vary)

Stories will vary.

© 1996 Kelley Wingate Publications   27   KW 1203

Page 28

Name _____   Skill: Story Web

| Stories have a beginning, a middle, and an end. |

Finish the story web. Use the words in the web to write a story about
the picture. Be sure to use capitals and periods. Think of a title for your story.

Things To Think About
Who is this story about? Where does this story take place? How does
this story begin? What happens next? How will you make this story end?

boots   umbrella
raincoat   rain   **puddle**
wet   **storm**
(Words will vary)

Stories will vary.

© 1996 Kelley Wingate Publications   28   KW 1203

Answer Key

Name _____ Skill: Story Web

Stories have a beginning, a middle, and an end.

Finish the story web. Use the words in the web to write a story about the picture. Be sure to use capitals and periods. Think of a title for your story.

Things To Think About
Who is this story about? Where does this story take place? How does this story begin? What happens next? How will you make this story end?

water | sunlight
seed — plant — stem
flower | pot
(words will vary)

_____

Stories will vary.

29   KW 1203

Name _____ Skill: Story Web

Stories have a beginning, a middle, and an end.

Finish the story web. Use the words in the web to write a story about the picture. Be sure to use capitals and periods. Think of a title for your story.

Things To Think About
Who is this story about? Where does this story take place? How does this story begin? What happens next? How will you make this story end?

swim | pool
happy — Water Park — slide
race | splash
(words will vary)

_____

Stories will vary.

30   KW 1203

Name _____ Skill: Constructing Stories

Stories have a beginning, a middle, and an end.

Write 5 sentences about this picture. Use the boxes at the end of each line to number your sentences in story order. Write your story. Title the story. Be sure to use capitals and periods.

1. I saw a big puddle. [2]
2. I was soaking wet! [5]
3. I stuck my toe in. [3]
4. It rained last night. [1]
5. I fell in. [4]

Things To Think About
Who is this story about? Where does this story take place? How does this story begin? What happens next? How will you make this story end?

_____

Wet From Head to Toe

It rained and rained last night. This morning I looked out of the window. I saw a big puddle in the front yard. I went outside and stuck my toe in the puddle. I lost my balance and fell in the water. I was soaking wet from head to toe!

31   KW 1203

Name _____ Skill: Constructing Stories

Stories have a beginning, a middle, and an end.

Write 5 sentences about this picture. Use the boxes at the end of each line to number your sentences in story order. Write your story. Title the story. Be sure to use capitals and periods.

1. Sentences will vary. [ ]
2. _____ [ ]
3. _____ [ ]
4. _____ [ ]
5. _____ [ ]

Things To Think About
Who is this story about? Where does this story take place? How does this story begin? What happens next? How will you make this story end?

_____

Stories will vary.

32   KW 1203

---

   110   CD-3718

Answer Key

Stories have a beginning, a middle, and an end.

Write 5 sentences about this picture. Use the boxes at the end of each line to number your sentences in story order. Write your story. Title the story. Be sure to use capitals and periods.

1. Sentences will vary. ☐
2. _____ ☐
3. _____ ☐
4. _____ ☐
5. _____ ☐

Things To Think About

Who is this story about? Where does this story take place? How does this story begin? What happens next? How will you make this story end?

_____

Stories will vary.

Stories have a beginning, a middle, and an end.

Write 5 sentences about this picture. Use the boxes at the end of each line to number your sentences in story order. Write your story. Title the story. Be sure to use capitals and periods.

1. Sentences will vary. ☐
2. _____ ☐
3. _____ ☐
4. _____ ☐
5. _____ ☐

Things To Think About

Who is this story about? Where does this story take place? How does this story begin? What happens next? How will you make this story end?

_____

Stories will vary.

Stories have a beginning, a middle, and an end.

Write 5 sentences about this picture. Use the boxes at the end of each line to number your sentences in story order. Write your story. Title the story. Be sure to use capitals and periods.

1. Sentences will vary. ☐
2. _____ ☐
3. _____ ☐
4. _____ ☐
5. _____ ☐

Things To Think About

Who is this story about? Where does this story take place? How does this story begin? What happens next? How will you make this story end?

_____

Stories will vary.

Stories have a beginning, a middle, and an end.

Write 5 sentences about this picture. Use the boxes at the end of each line to number your sentences in story order. Write your story. Title the story. Be sure to use capitals and periods.

1. Sentences will vary. ☐
2. _____ ☐
3. _____ ☐
4. _____ ☐
5. _____ ☐

Things To Think About

Who is this story about? Where does this story take place? How does this story begin? What happens next? How will you make this story end?

_____

Stories will vary.

Answer Key

Name _____   Skill: Writing Stories

Stories have a beginning, a middle, and an end.

Write a story about the picture. Add your own ending. Be sure to use capitals and periods. Title your story.

Things To Think About
Who is this story about? Where does this story take place? How does this story begin? What happens next? How will you make this story end?

Token

Aunt Jill lives in New York City. She rides the subway every day. A subway is a train that travels underground in a tunnel. One day Aunt Jill was riding home from work, she heard a "meow". There was a kitten under her seat. It looked hungry and frightened. Aunt Jill put the kitten in her pocket. She took it home with her. She named the kitten Token. Now, the kitten is a fat fluffy cat. It runs to the door to greet Aunt Jill when she comes home every day.

Name _____   Skill: Writing Stories

Stories have a beginning, a middle, and an end.

Write a story about the picture. Add your own ending. Be sure to use capitals and periods. Title your story.

Things To Think About
Who is this story about? Where does this story take place? How does this story begin? What happens next? How will you make this story end?

Stories will vary.

Name _____   Skill: Writing Stories

Stories have a beginning, a middle, and an end.

Write a story about the picture. Add your own ending. Be sure to use capitals and periods. Title your story.

Things To Think About
Who is this story about? Where does this story take place? How does this story begin? What happens next? How will you make this story end?

Stories will vary.

Name _____   Skill: Writing Stories

Stories have a beginning, a middle, and an end.

Write a story about the picture. Add your own ending. Be sure to use capitals and periods. Title your story.

Things To Think About
Who is this story about? Where does this story take place? How does this story begin? What happens next? How will you make this story end?

Stories will vary.

Answer Key

Name _____   Skill: Writing Stories

Stories have a beginning, a middle, and an end.

Write a story about the picture. Add your own ending. Be sure to use capitals and periods. Title your story.

Things To Think About

Who is this story about? Where does this story take place? How does this story begin? What happens next? How will you make this story end?

_____

Stories will vary.

Name _____   Skill: Writing Stories

Stories have a beginning, a middle, and an end.

Write a story about the picture. Add your own ending. Be sure to use capitals and periods. Title your story.

Things To Think About

Who is this story about? Where does this story take place? How does this story begin? What happens next? How will you make this story end?

_____

Stories will vary.

Name _____   Skill: Writing Paragraphs

A paragraph contains a main idea and supporting details.

Every paragraph has one main idea. The main idea is called the **topic sentence**. It is usually the first sentence in the paragraph. The other sentences are **details** that tell more about the main idea. The last sentence retells the main idea.

1. Read over the main idea and details listed below.

Title of paragraph: My Mom

Main Idea: My mom is the best!

Details:
1. She gives me hugs and kisses.
2. She helps me with my homework.
3. She cooks great dinners.
4. She takes me shopping.

Retell Main Idea: I think my mom is wonderful.

2. Use these sentences to write a paragraph. Write the main idea, add the details, then retell the main idea. Indent the first sentence. Use capitals and periods. Remember to give the paragraph a title.

My Mom

My mom is the best! She always gives me lots of hugs and kisses. She helps me with my homework if there is something I don't understand. She cooks great dinners. Sometimes on Saturday she takes me shopping. I think my mom is wonderful.

Name _____   Skill: Writing Paragraphs

A paragraph contains a main idea and supporting details.

Every paragraph has one main idea. The main idea is called the **topic sentence**. It is usually the first sentence in the paragraph. The other sentences are **details** that tell more about the main idea. The last sentence retells the main idea.

1. Read over the main idea and details listed below.

Title of paragraph: Washing My Hair

Main Idea: I wash my hair at least four times a week.

Details:
1. I get in the shower.
2. I wet my hair.
3. I pour shampoo on my head.
4. I rinse my hair well.

Retell Main Idea: Now I have clean hair.

2. Use these sentences to write a paragraph. Write the main idea, add the details, then retell the main idea. Indent the first sentence. Use capitals and periods. Remember to give the paragraph a title.

_____

Stories will vary.

Answer Key

Name _____   Skill: Writing Paragraphs

| A paragraph contains a main idea and supporting details. |

Every paragraph has one main idea. The main idea is called the **topic sentence**. It is usually the first sentence in the paragraph. The other sentences are **details** that tell more about the main idea. The last sentence retells the main idea.

1. Read over the title and main idea of the paragraph. Write your own details.

Title of paragraph: <u>Making Toast</u>

Main Idea: Toast is easy to make.

Details: 1. *Sentences will vary.*
        2. _____
        3. _____
        4. _____

Retell Main Idea: It is not hard to make toast.

2. Use these sentences to write a paragraph. Write the main idea, add the details, then retell the main idea. Indent the first sentence. Use capitals and periods. Remember to give the paragraph a title.

_____

Stories will vary.

Name _____   Skill: Writing Paragraphs

| A paragraph contains a main idea and supporting details. |

Every paragraph has one main idea. The main idea is called the **topic sentence**. It is usually the first sentence in the paragraph. The other sentences are **details** that tell more about the main idea. The last sentence retells the main idea.

2. Look at the title and main idea of the paragraph. Write your own details.

Title of paragraph: <u>Playing Baseball</u>

Main Idea: Baseball is an exciting game to play!

Details: 1. *Sentences will vary.*
        2. _____
        3. _____
        4. _____

Retell Main Idea: Do you see why I love baseball?

2. Use these sentences to write a paragraph. Write the main idea, add the details, then retell the main idea. Indent the first sentence. Use capitals and periods. Remember to give the paragraph a title.

_____

Stories will vary.

Name _____   Skill: Writing Paragraphs

| A paragraph contains a main idea and supporting details. |

Every paragraph has one main idea. The main idea is called the **topic sentence**. It is usually the first sentence in the paragraph. The other sentences are **details** that tell more about the main idea. The last sentence retells the main idea.

1. Look at the title and main idea of the paragraph. Write your own details.

Title of paragraph: <u>Birthdays</u>

Main Idea: Birthdays are fun.

Details: 1. *Sentences will vary.*
        2. _____
        3. _____
        4. _____

Retell Main Idea: I wish my birthday came more often.

2. Use these sentences to write a paragraph. Write the main idea, add the details, then retell the main idea. Indent the first sentence. Use capitals and periods. Remember to give the paragraph a title.

_____

Stories will vary.

Name _____   Skill: Writing Paragraphs

| A paragraph contains a main idea and supporting details. |

Every paragraph has one main idea. The main idea is called the **topic sentence**. It is usually the first sentence in the paragraph. The other sentences are **details** that tell more about the main idea. The last sentence retells the main idea.

1. Look at the title and main idea of the paragraph. Write your own details.

Title of paragraph: <u>My Favorite Lunch</u>

Main Idea: Hamburgers and french fries are my favorite lunch.

Details: 1. *Sentences will vary.*
        2. _____
        3. _____
        4. _____

Retell Main Idea: I would chose them for lunch any day!

2. Use these sentences to write a paragraph. Write the main idea, add the details, then retell the main idea. Indent the first sentence. Use capitals and periods. Remember to give the paragraph a title.

_____

Stories will vary.

Answer Key

Name _____   Skill: Writing Paragraphs

| A paragraph contains a main idea and supporting details. |

Every paragraph has one main idea. The main idea is called the **topic sentence**. It is usually the first sentence in the paragraph. The other sentences are **details** that tell more about the main idea. The last sentence retells the main idea.

1. Choose an idea for your paragraph. Write the title, main idea, and details. Retell the main idea at the end.

Title of paragraph: _____

Main Idea: _____

Details: 1. _Sentences will vary._

2. _____

3. _____

4. _____

Retell Main Idea: _____

2. Use these sentences to write a paragraph. Write the main idea, add the details, then retell the main idea. Indent the first sentence. Use capitals and periods. Remember to give the paragraph a title.

Stories will vary.

_____

_____

_____

_____

© 1996 Kelley Wingate Publications   49   KW 1203

Name _____   Skill: Persuasive Paragraphs

| A paragraph contains a main idea and supporting details. |

Some paragraphs are written to persuade, or change the way people think. These paragraphs have a main idea and supporting details.

1. You must convince your mom to let you walk to the store to buy an apple. Give your reasons. Then ask again.

Title :   _Apple_

Question: May I walk to the store and buy an apple?

Reasons: 1. I will be careful crossing the street.
2. I have my own money to buy the apple.
3. It is early, so I will still be hungry for dinner.
4. I will help you set the table when I get back.

Ask again: Is it all right for me to go to the store?

2. Use these sentences to write a paragraph. Write the main ideas, add the details, then retell the main idea. Indent the first sentence. Use capitals and periods. Remember to give the paragraph a title.

Apple
May I walk to the store and buy an apple? I will use my own money to buy it. It is early, so I will still be hungry for dinner. I will help you set the table when I get back. Is it all right for me to go to the store?

© 1996 Kelley Wingate Publications   50   KW 1203

Name _____   Skill: Persuasive Paragraphs

| A paragraph contains a main idea and supporting details. |

Some paragraphs are written to persuade, or change the way people think. These paragraphs have a main idea and supporting details.

1. You must convince your teacher to let you change your desk from the front to the back of the room. Give your reasons. Then ask again.

Title :   _Changing Desks_

Question: May I move my desk to the back of the classroom?

Reasons: 1. I will work better in the back of the room.
2. No one will bother me in the back of the class.
3. It is quieter in the back of the room.
4. I am too tall to sit in the front.

Ask again: May I move to the back of the room?

2. Use these sentences to write a paragraph. Write the main idea, add the details, then retell the main idea. Indent the first sentence. Use capitals and periods. Remember to give the paragraph a title.

_____

Stories will vary.

_____

_____

_____

_____

_____

© 1996 Kelley Wingate Publications   51   KW 1203

Name _____   Skill: Persuasive Paragraphs

| A paragraph contains a main idea and supporting details. |

Some paragraphs are written to persuade, or change the way people think. These paragraphs have a main idea and supporting details.

1. You must convince your mom and dad to let you have a puppy. Give your reasons. Then ask again.

Title : _____

Question: May I

Reasons: 1. _Answers will vary._
2. _____
3. _____
4. _____

Ask again: _____

2. Use these sentences to write a paragraph. Write the main idea, add the details, then retell the main idea. Indent the first sentence. Use capitals and periods. Remember to give the paragraph a title.

_____

Stories will vary.

_____

_____

_____

_____

_____

© 1996 Kelley Wingate Publications   52   KW 1203

Answer Key

Page 53

Name _____ Skill: Persuasive Paragraphs

A paragraph contains a main idea and supporting details.

Some paragraphs are written to persuade, or change the way people think. These paragraphs have a main idea and supporting details.

1. You must convince your mom to let you play in the rain. Give your reasons. Then ask again.

Title : _____

Question: May I _____

Reasons: 1. Answers will vary.
2. _____
3. _____
4. _____

Ask again: _____

2. Use these sentences to write a paragraph.. Write the main idea, add the details, then retell the main idea. Indent the first sentence. Use capitals and periods. Remember to give the paragraph a title.

_____

Stories will vary.

© 1996 Kelley Wingate Publications   53   KW 1203

Page 54

Name _____ Skill: Persuasive Paragraphs

A paragraph contains a main idea and supporting details.

Some paragraphs are written to persuade, or change the way people think. These paragraphs have a main idea and supporting details.

1. You must convince your mom to buy you a bike for your birthday. Give your reasons. Then ask again.

Title : _____

Question: May I _____

Reasons: 1. Answers will vary.
2. _____
3. _____
4. _____

Ask again: _____

2. Use these sentences to write a paragraph. Write the main idea, add the details, then retell the main idea. Indent the first sentence. Use capitals and periods. Remember to give the paragraph a title.

_____

Stories will vary.

© 1996 Kelley Wingate Publications   54   KW 1203

Page 55

Name _____ Skill: Persuasive Paragraphs

A paragraph contains a main idea and supporting details.

Some paragraphs are written to persuade, or change the way people think. These paragraphs have a main idea and supporting details.

1. You must convince your mom to let you play at a friend's house. Give your reasons. Then ask again.

Title : _____

Question: May I _____

Reasons: 1. Answers will vary.
2. _____
3. _____
4. _____

Ask again: _____

2. Use these sentences to write a paragraph. Write the main idea, add the details, then retell the main idea. Indent the first sentence. Use capitals and periods. Remember to give the paragraph a title.

_____

Stories will vary.

© 1996 Kelley Wingate Publications   55   KW 1203

Page 56

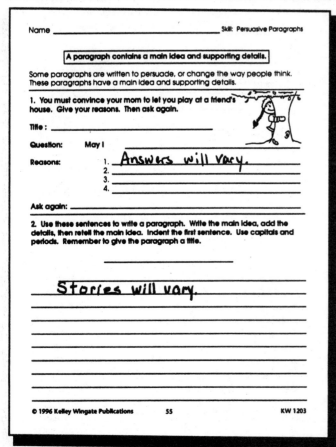

Name _____ · Skill: Invitations

An invitation includes all the important facts.

"You are invited!" You must know why, who, when, and, where. An invitation gives you all this information.

1. Read the invitation and answer the questions.

Halloween Party!

Given by: Tony Black
Time: 7:00 p.m.
Date: October 31
Place: 420 Apple Street

Why has the invitation been sent?
Halloween Party

Who is giving the party?
Tony Black

When will you go?
October 31 7:00 p.m.

Where will you go?
420 Apple Street

2. Make a birthday invitation. List the important information. Write the information on the invitation.

Why will the invitation be sent?
Answers will vary.

Who is giving the party?
_____

When is the party?
_____

Where is the party?
_____

You're Invited!

COME _____

Given by: _____
Time: _____
Date: _____
Place: _____

© 1996 Kelley Wingate Publications   56   KW 1203

Answer Key

Name _____ Skill: Invitations

An invitation includes all the important facts.

"You are invited!" You must know <u>why, who, when, and where</u>.
An invitation gives you all this information.

1. **Read the invitation and answer the questions.**

★★★★★★★★★★★★★★★
Grand Opening!
Given by: Bob's Toy Store
Time: 10:00 a.m.
Date: June 14
Place: 856 Main Street

<u>Why</u> has the invitation been sent?
Grand Opening
<u>Who</u> is having the grand opening?
Bob's Toy Store
<u>When</u> will you go?
June 14 10:00 a.m.
<u>Where</u> will you go?
856 Main Street

2. **Write an invitation to a new park called Play Land. List the important information. Write the information on the invitation.**

<u>Why</u> will the invitation be sent?
Answers will vary.
<u>Who</u> is giving the party?
_____
<u>When</u> is the party?
_____
<u>Where</u> is the party?
_____

You're Invited!
COME _____
Given by: _____
Time: _____
Date: _____
Place: _____

© 1996 Kelley Wingate Publications   57   KW 1203

Name _____ Skill: Invitations

An invitation includes all the important facts.

"You are invited!" You must know <u>why, who, when, and where</u>.
An invitation gives you all this information.

1. **Read the invitation and answer the questions.**

Come to Our Class Play!
Given by: Mrs. Bar's 3rd Grade Class
Time: 2:00 p.m.
Date: December 15
Place: Martin Elementary School

<u>Why</u> has the invitation been sent?
Class Play
<u>Who</u> is giving the play?
Mrs. Bar's Class
<u>When</u> will you go?
December 15 2:00 p.m.
<u>Where</u> will you go?
Martin Elementary School

2. **Write an invitation to a parents meeting at school. List the important information. Write the information on the invitation.**

<u>Why</u> will the invitation be sent?
Answers will vary.
<u>Who</u> is giving the party?
_____
<u>When</u> is the party?
_____
<u>Where</u> is the party?
_____

You're Invited!
COME _____
Given by: _____
Time: _____
Date: _____
Place: _____

© 1996 Kelley Wingate Publications   58   KW 1203

Name _____ Skill: Invitations

An invitation includes all the important facts.

"You are invited!" You must know <u>why, who, when, and where</u>.
An invitation gives you all this information.

1. **Read the invitation and answer the questions.**

Pet Show!
Given by: The City Pet Shelter
Time: 9:00 a.m.
Date: May 9
Place: 127 Kitten Street

<u>Why</u> has the invitation been sent?
Pet Show
<u>Who</u> is giving the show?
City Pet Shelter
<u>When</u> will you go?
May 9 9:00 a.m.
<u>Where</u> will you go?
127 Kitten Street

2. **Write an invitation to a school fair. List the important information. Write the information on the invitation.**

<u>Why</u> will the invitation be sent?
Answers will vary.
<u>Who</u> is giving the party?
_____
<u>When</u> is the party?
_____
<u>Where</u> is the party?
_____

You're Invited!
COME _____
Given by: _____
Time: _____
Date: _____
Place: _____

© 1996 Kelley Wingate Publications   59   KW 1203

Name _____ Skill: Invitations

An invitation includes all the important facts.

"You are invited!" You must know <u>why, who, when, and where</u>.
An invitation gives you all this information.

1. **Read the invitation and answer the questions.**

Dinner Party!
Given by: Anne Winters
Time: 7:00 p.m.
Date: November 27
Place: 608 Lake Drive

<u>Why</u> has the invitation been sent?
Dinner Party
<u>Who</u> is giving the party?
Anne Winters
<u>When</u> will you go?
November 27 7:00 p.m.
<u>Where</u> will you go?
608 Lake Drive

2. **Write an invitation to a skating party. List the important information. Write the information on the invitation.**

<u>Why</u> will the invitation be sent?
Answers will vary.
<u>Who</u> is giving the party?
_____
<u>When</u> is the party?
_____
<u>Where</u> is the party?
_____

You're Invited!
COME _____
Given by: _____
Time: _____
Date: _____
Place: _____

© 1996 Kelley Wingate Publications   60   KW 1203

Answer Key

Name _____ Skill: Invitations

An invitation includes all the important facts.

"You are invited!" You must know <u>why, who, when, and where</u>.
An invitation gives you all this information.

1. Make your own invitation and illustrate it. Answer the questions.

_____	<u>Why</u> has the invitation been sent?
	Answers will vary.
Given by: _____	<u>Who</u> is giving the party?
Time: _____	
Date: _____	<u>When</u> will you go?
Place: _____	<u>Where</u> will you go?

2. Make your own invitation. List the important information. Write the information on the invitation.

<u>Why</u> will the invitation be sent?
Answers will vary.
<u>Who</u> is giving the party?
_____
<u>When</u> is the party?
_____
<u>Where</u> is the party?
_____

You're Invited!

_____
Given by: _____
Time: _____
Date: _____
Place: _____

© 1996 Kelley Wingate Publications   61   KW 1203

Name _____ Skill: Friendly Letters

A friendly letter has 5 parts: date, greeting, body, closing, and signature.

greeting → Dear Tim,

July 10, 1996 ← date

body → What a great time we had when you came to visit. I liked playing baseball and football with you. Swimming was fun, too.
I hope you will come to visit me again soon.

Your friend, ← closing
Jason ← signature

Write a letter to your friend. Talk about things you like to do together.

_____ (date)
(greeting)
Letters will vary.
_____
_____
(body)
(closing)
(signature)

© 1996 Kelley Wingate Publications   62   KW 1203

Name _____ Skill: Friendly Letters

A friendly letter has 5 parts: date, greeting, body, closing, and signature.

1. Read these letter parts. Rewrite each part in the proper place on the letter form at the right.

Dear Aunt Carol,

Amanda

February 3

Love,

   Thank you for the new red shirt you sent for my birthday. I really love it. I will wear it to school on Monday.

February 3
(date)
Dear Aunt Carol,
(greeting)
Thank you for the new red shirt you sent for my birthday. I really love it. I will wear it to school on Monday.

Love,
(closing)
Amanda
(signature)

2. Write a letter to your grandmother. Thank her for the gift she sent you. Be sure to put a comma after the greeting and closing.

_____
Letters will vary.
_____
_____
_____

© 1996 Kelley Wingate Publications   63   KW 1203

Name _____ Skill: Friendly Letters

A friendly letter has 5 parts: date, greeting, body, closing, and signature.

1. Write a letter to your teacher. Thank her for taking you on a field trip. Include all 5 parts of a letter. Be sure to put a comma after the greeting and closing.

_____
Letters will vary.
_____
_____
_____

2. Write a letter to your classmate. Ask him to come to your house on Saturday. Write about the things you will do when he comes.

_____
Letters will vary.
_____
_____
_____

© 1996 Kelley Wingate Publications   64   KW 1203

Answer Key

Name _____   Skill: Friendly Letters

A friendly letter has 5 parts: date, greeting, body, closing, and signature.

Write a letter to your new friend.

Describe yourself.

Letters will vary.

Tell what you like to do.

Describe your room.

Describe your family.

© 1996 Kelley Wingate Publications   65   KW 1203

Name _____   Skill: Friendly Letters

A friendly letter has 5 parts: date, greeting, body, closing, and signature.

1. Write a letter to a firefighter. What would you like to ask her?
1. Questions will vary.
2. _____
3. _____
4. _____
5. _____

2. Use the above questions to write your letter.

Letters will vary.

© 1996 Kelley Wingate Publications   66   KW 1203

Name _____   Skill: Friendly Letters

A friendly letter has 5 parts: date, greeting, body, closing, and signature.

Write a letter to someone you know.

Letters will vary.

© 1996 Kelley Wingate Publications   67   KW 1203

Name _____   Skill: Addressing Envelopes

It is important to address an envelope correctly. An envelope shows who is sending a letter and who is receiving a letter. Name, address, city, state, and zip code must be placed in the proper places.

The sender is : A
His house address is : B
His city, state, and zip code are : C

The receiver is : D
His house address is : E
His city, state, and zip code are : F

1. Study the completed envelope.

A → Mr. John Bacon
B → 715 North Street
C → Newton, LA   39245

D → Mr. Ken Brown
E → 18 Beach Road
F → Austin, TX   70792

2. Address the envelope below with the information given.

The sender is:
Miss Karen Taylor
562 Clover Road
Jackson, MS 44823

The receiver is:
Mrs. Donna Burns
74 Valley Street
Buffalo, NY 48704

A → Miss Karen Taylor
B → 562 Clover Road
C → Jackson, MS 44823

D → Mrs. Donna Burns
E → 74 Valley Street
F → Buffalo, NY 48704

© 1996 Kelley Wingate Publications   68   KW 1203

Answer Key

Name _____ Skill: Addressing Envelopes

It is important to address an envelope correctly. An envelope shows who is sending a letter and who is receiving a letter. Name, address, city, state, and zip code must be placed in the proper places.

1. Address the envelope below with the information given.

The sender is:
Dr. James Madison
38 Carlton Place
Salem, NC 89532

The receiver is:
Ms. Mary Morton
149 Sparrow Street
Tucson, AZ 52974

Dr. James Madison
38 Carlton Place
Salem, NC 89532

Ms. Mary Morton
149 Sparrow Street
Tucson, AZ 52974

2. Address the envelope below with the information given.

The sender is:
Mrs. Alice Wilson
9 Flag Avenue
Port Huron, MI 48060

The receiver is:
Miss Susan Coats
183 Spring Street
Denver, CO 50738

Mrs. Alice Wilson
9 Flag Avenue
Port Huron, MI 48060

Miss Susan Coats
183 Spring Street
Denver, CO 50738

© 1996 Kelley Wingate Publications   69   KW 1203

Name _____ Skill: Addressing Envelopes

It is important to address an envelope correctly. An envelope shows who is sending a letter and who is receiving a letter. Name, address, city, state, and zip code must be placed in the proper places.

1. Address the envelope below with the information given.

The sender is:
Mr. Martin Guy
77 Troy Avenue
Toronto, Ontario M9L 1Z1

The receiver is:
Mrs. Cindy Lesson
293 Park Place
Conner, RI 24375

Mr. Martin Guy
77 Troy Avenue
Toronto, Ontario M9L 1Z1

Mrs. Cindy Lesson
293 Park Place
Conner, RI 24375

2. Address the envelope below with the information given.

The sender is:
Ms. Lynn Sprat
14 Woods Drive
Miami, FL 66931

The receiver is:
Miss Lisa Kent
941 York Street
Madison, WI 22814

Ms. Lynn Sprat
14 Woods Drive
Miami, FL 66931

Miss Lisa Kent
941 York Street
Madison, WI 22814

© 1996 Kelley Wingate Publications   70   KW 1203

Name _____ Skill: Addressing Envelopes

It is important to address an envelope correctly. An envelope shows who is sending a letter and who is receiving a letter. Name, address, city, state, and zip code must be placed in the proper places.

1. Address the envelope below with the information given.

The sender is:
Dr. Joe Scott
253 Forest Lane
Atlanta, GA 34274

The receiver is:
Mr. Alan Smith
174 Star Road
Salem, OR 69274

Dr. Joe Scott
253 Forest Lane
Atlanta, GA 34274

Mr. Alan Smith
174 Star Road
Salem, OR 69274

2. Address the envelope below with the information given.

The sender is:
Mr. Don Davis
33 Leland Place
Wheeling, PA 81475

The receiver is:
Mrs. Sharon Keys
590 Broad Street
Tulsa, OK 42851

Mr. Don Davis
33 Leland Place
Wheeling, PA 81475

Mrs. Sharon Keys
590 Broad Street
Tulsa, OK 42851

© 1996 Kelley Wingate Publications   71   KW 1203

Name _____ Skill: Addressing Envelopes

It is important to address an envelope correctly. An envelope shows who is sending a letter and who is receiving a letter. Name, address, city, state, and zip code must be placed in the proper places.

1. Address this envelope to someone you know.

Envelopes will vary.

2. Address this envelope to someone you know.

Envelopes will vary.

© 1996 Kelley Wingate Publications   72   KW 1203

Answer Key

Name _____ Skill: Descriptive Writing

Adjectives are words that describe which, how many,
what color, and what an object looks or feels like.

Adjectives make stories more colorful and interesting.
They help you "see" a story in your imagination.

For each picture below list 4 adjectives to describe it. Write a paragraph about
each picture. Use your adjectives. Write a title for your paragraph.

1. tropical 2. juicy
3. round 4. golden

Juicy Fruits

Fruit is not only juicy, but delicious.
Red, ripe watermelon tastes sweet and
yummy. Round oranges and golden
pineapple make great snacks. They
can also be squeezed into tasty
drinks. Tropical fruits make any day great.

1. small 2. puffy
3. white 4. neat
(words will vary)

Paragraphs will vary.

Name _____ Skill: Descriptive Writing

Adjectives are words that describe which, how many,
what color, and what an object looks or feels like.

Adjectives make stories more colorful and interesting.
They help you "see" a story in your imagination.

For each picture below list 4 adjectives to describe it. Write a paragraph about
each picture. Use your adjectives. Write a title for your paragraph.

(words will vary)
1. wet 2. deep
3. rainy 4. yellow

Paragraphs will vary.

1. fuzzy 2. warm
3. brown 4. soft
(words will vary)

Paragraphs will vary.

Name _____ Skill: Descriptive Writing

Adjectives are words that describe which, how many,
what color, and what an object looks or feels like.

Adjectives make stories more colorful and interesting.
They help you "see" a story in your imagination.

1. Read the following paragraph.
   I have a favorite pair of shoes. They are old. My mom doesn't like them.
She wants me to throw them away and get a new pair. I would rather keep my
old shoes.

2. Now, read the same paragraph with adjectives and more description
added.
   I have a favorite pair of shoes. They are old and comfortable. The shoes
are blue and white. The left shoe has a hole in the toe, and the right has a
broken shoelace. Both of them have holes worn in the bottom. My mom
doesn't like my old shoes. They are very dirty. She wants me to throw them
away and get a new pair. I would rather keep my old, comfy, worn out shoes.

3. Read the following paragraph then make it more interesting. Use adjectives
to rewrite it.
   Yesterday my family took a train ride. There was an engine, passenger
cars, and box cars. A caboose was at the end. The whistle blew. We were off!
Smoke blew from the engine. The cars began to rock. I would like to ride on a
train again.

Yesterday my family took an exciting
train ride. There was a large, black
engine, comfortable passenger cars, and
sixteen box cars. A bright red
caboose was at the end. The loud
whistle blew. We were off! Gray smoke
blew from the puffing engine. The
cars began to rock. I would like to
ride on a train again.

Name _____ Skill: Descriptive Writing

Adjectives are words that describe which, how many,
what color, and what an object looks or feels like.

Adjectives make stories more colorful and interesting.
They help you "see" a story in your imagination.

1. Read the following paragraph.
   I like to watch the sunset. The colors are beautiful. Sometimes the sun
peeks through the clouds and makes more colors. As the sun sinks, the sky
becomes darker. Soon night will be here and stars will come out.

2. Now, read the same paragraph with adjectives and more description
added.
   I like to watch the sunset. The red and orange colors are beautiful.
Sometimes the sun peeks between clouds, turning them pink and purple. As
the sun sinks, the evening sky becomes a dark blue then black. Soon the inky
night sky will shine with bright stars.

3. Read the following paragraph then make it more interesting. Use adjectives
to rewrite it.
   My sister and I went for a walk in the forest. We came to a gingerbread
house. I thought it looked very strange. My sister thought it looked tasty. We
will never forget that house in the woods.

Paragraphs will vary.

Answer Key

Name _____   Skill: Descriptive Writing

> Adjectives are words that describe which, how many, what color, and what an object looks or feels like.

Adjectives make stories more colorful and interesting. They help you "see" a story in your imagination.

1. Read this paragraph.
   I live in a house. It is built out of bricks. There is a fence around the yard. I planted flowers in the gardens. My house looks pretty.

2. This is the same paragraph with adjectives and more description added.
   I live in a small, neat house. It is built out of brown and white bricks. There is a tall, wooden fence around the large yard. I planted beautiful red and yellow flowers in the front and back gardens. My little house looks pretty.

3. Read this paragraph then make it more interesting. Use adjectives to rewrite it.
   Winter is here. All the trees are bare. It is cold outside. Children are wearing warm clothes. Smoke rises from chimneys. Soon it will be snowing. Everything will be covered in snow. It is time for plants and some animals to go to sleep for the winter. Winter is a nice season.

Paragraphs will vary.

© 1996 Kelley Wingate Publications   77   KW 1203

Name _____   Skill: Compare and Contrast

> Some things can be both alike and different.

1. Fill in the blanks with words that tell how a tree and flower are alike and different. The first one has been done for you.

          tree   flower
   different   alike   different

1. Trunk	1. Roots	1. Stem
2. Branches	2. Leaves	2. Petals
3. Nests	3. Plants	3. Blossoms

(answers will vary)

2. Write two paragraphs below. In the first paragraph tell how trees and flowers are alike. Tell how each is different in the second paragraph. Title your story.

Trees and Flowers

   Both trees and flowers are plants. They each have roots and leaves. Trees and flowers need air, water, and sunlight. They both make oxygen. Trees and flowers make the earth beautiful.
   Trees have strong, thick trunks. They sprout branches. Birds build their nests in these branches. Flowers have thin breakable stems. They sprout blossoms made out of petals. Flowers can be picked for boquets.

© 1996 Kelley Wingate Publications   78   KW 1203

Name _____   Skill: Compare and Contrast

> Some things can be both alike and different.

1. Fill in the blanks with words that tell how a cat and a dog are alike and different. The first one has been done for you.

          cat   dog
   different   alike   different

1. pointed ears	1. furry	1. floppy ears
2. long tail	2. pets	2. short tail
3. meows	3. animal	3. barks

(answers will vary)

2. Write two paragraphs below. In the first paragraph tell how cats and dogs are alike. Tell how each is different in the second paragraph. Title your story.

_____

Paragraphs will vary.

© 1996 Kelley Wingate Publications   79   KW 1203

Name _____   Skill: Compare and Contrast

> Some things can be both alike and different.

1. Fill in the blanks with words that tell how lettuce and carrots are alike and different. The first one has been done for you.

          lettuce   carrots
   different   alike   different

1. green	1. vegetables	1. orange
2. leafy	2. green leaves	2. pointed
3. thin	3. we eat them	3. round

(answers will vary)

2. Write two paragraphs below. In the first paragraph tell how lettuce and carrots are alike. Tell how each is different in the second paragraph. Title your story.

_____

Paragraphs will vary.

© 1996 Kelley Wingate Publications   80   KW 1203

Answer Key

Name _____   Skill: Compare and Contrast

Some things can be both alike and different.

1. Fill in the blanks with words that tell how a watch and a clock are alike and different. The first one has been done for you.

watch   clock

different   alike   different

1. has a wrist band   1. both have hands   1. has a base
2. Wear it   2. round face   2. has alarm
3. Smaller   3. numbers   3. larger
                 (answers will vary)

2. Write two paragraphs below. In the first paragraph tell how watches and clocks are alike. Tell how each is different in the second paragraph. Title your story.

_____

Paragraphs will vary.

81   KW 1203

Name _____   Skill: Compare and Contrast

Some things can be both alike and different.

1. Fill in the lines with words that tell how corn and a banana are alike and different.

banana   corn

different   alike   different

1. fruit   1. yellow   1. vegetable
2. in a bunch   2. long + round 2. in ears
3. grows on tree 3. we eat them   3. grows on stalk
                 (answers will vary)

2. Write two paragraphs below. In the first paragraph tell how bananas and corn are alike. Tell how each is different in the second paragraph. Title your story.

_____

Paragraphs will vary.

82   KW 1203

Name _____   Skill: Proofing for Punctuation

A sentence ends in a punctuation mark.

1. Place the correct punctuation mark at the end of each sentence. Add an ending to the story.

Digging For Worms

Once upon a time there was a boy named Jake. Jake and his mother were very poor and hungry. One day Jake was digging for worms to eat. He dug and dug. Soon he was in a deep hole. It was so deep that he could not climb out. Suddenly a giant worm stuck his head out of the dirt at the bottom of the hole! Jake was frightened. He looked at the worm and

Endings will vary.

2. Write your own story about giant worms. Use correct punctuation.

_____

Stories will vary.

83   KW 1203

Name _____   Skill: Proofing for Punctuation

A sentence ends in a punctuation mark.

1. Place the correct punctuation mark at the end of each sentence. Add an ending to the story.

Backwards-Inside-Out Day

Today is a "Backwards-Inside-Out-Day" at school. Everyone must come to school with their clothes on backwards and inside-out. Shirts and pants must be worn backwards. Sweaters and belts should be on backwards. Everything is turned inside-out. Some things cannot be worn backwards or inside-out. You can't wear your shoes backwards. What do we do then? We wear things that don't match. I will wear one black shoe and one red shoe. I think my teacher

Endings will vary.

2. What would you wear on "Backward-Inside-Out" day? Use correct punctuation.

_____

Stories will vary.

84   KW 1203

Answer Key

© 1996 Kelley Wingate Publications   124   CD-3718

Worksheet 1 (page 85):

Name _____   Skill: Proofing for Punctuation

A sentence ends in a punctuation mark.

1. Place the correct punctuation mark at the end of each sentence.
Add an ending to the story.

Making Pancakes

My sister and I woke up early last Saturday morning. We decided to make breakfast for Mom. We took out the pancake mix. We put the mix in a big bowl. We added eggs and milk. I was stirring the batter. My sister was pouring orange juice. Just then the cat jumped up onto the counter. He tipped over the glass of juice and knocked the bowl to the floor. Batter and juice were everywhere! Just then

Endings will vary.

2. Write about something you have cooked. Use correct punctuation.

Stories will vary.

© 1996 Kelley Wingate Publications   85   KW 1203

Worksheet 2 (page 86):

Name _____   Skill: Proofing for Punctuation

Sentences and proper nouns begin with capital letters.

Place capital letters where they are needed. Add an ending to the story.

A stormy night

It was a stormy, dark, October night. Robin and I were frightened. The wind was whistling through the trees. Lightening flashes danced off the windows. Thunder was rumbling across the sky. We were all alone in the house. Mom and Dad had gone to Aunt Jan's home for a dinner party. We hoped that they would be back soon. We always stayed up late on Saturday nights, but tonight we were already under the covers. Our dog, Taffy, was in bed with us. She was afraid, too. Just then we heard a knock at the door. "Who is it?" I called. We looked out the window and there stood

Endings will vary.

© 1996 Kelley Wingate Publications   86   KW 1203

Worksheet 3 (page 87):

Name _____   Skill: Proofing for Capitals

Sentences and proper nouns begin with capital letters.

Place capital letters where they are needed. Add an ending to the story.

My birthday

Today is my birthday. I am nine years old. I was born on Wednesday, April 12 in Billings, Montana. My family will celebrate my birthday tonight. Mom will cook her special spaghetti dinner just for me. Dad will be home from work early. My brother, David, and my sister, Rose, will be here, too. After dinner Grandma and Grandpa will come. We will all eat cake and ice cream. They will sing "Happy Birthday" to me. Then I

Endings will vary.

© 1996 Kelley Wingate Publications   87   KW 1203

Worksheet 4 (page 88):

Name _____   Skill: Proofing for Capitals

Sentences and proper nouns begin with capital letters.

Place capital letters where they are needed. Add an ending to the story.

The magic show

Aunt Gail took me to a magic show last Thursday afternoon. The show was held at the Adams Theater on River Road. The magician's name was Morton the Magnificent. Morton was wonderful! He made two birds disappear. He made a quarter appear from behind Frank Hopkin's ear. Morton made a flower out of paper. When he waved a wand over it, the flower became real. He asked Mr. Rogers to come up on stage. Morton made Mr. Rogers float through the air. Morton chose Aunt Gail for another trick. He put her into a long box so only her head and feet showed. He took a saw and began to cut the box in half. Aunt Gail screamed and I

Endings will vary.

© 1996 Kelley Wingate Publications   88   KW 1203

Answer Key

Worksheet 1 (page 89)

Name_____ Skill: Proof for Capitals and Punctuation

> Sentences need punctuation marks.
> Sentences and proper nouns begin with capital letters.

Place punctuation marks and capital letters where they are needed.
Add an ending to the story.

The Adventure of Baby Bird

Mother bird was busy with her three new babies. They were growing so quickly. Soon they would all begin flying. They were always hungry. She could never seem to find enough food to keep them full. Back and forth she flew all day long with worms and bugs.

Chirpy was the smallest of the three babies. He was also the bravest. He liked to jump to the edge of the nest to see his new world. Mother bird warned him to be careful. She said that he might fall from the nest. There were cats in the yard below. How would he get home if he fell out of the nest?

Mother bird flew away to get the babies their dinner. Chirpy hopped right up on the edge of the nest. Suddenly his foot slipped he began to fall

Endings will vary.

© 1996 Kelley Wingate Publications   89   KW 1203

Worksheet 2 (page 90)

Name_____ Skill: Proof for Capitals and Punctuation

> Sentences need punctuation marks.
> Sentences and proper nouns begin with capital letters.

Place punctuation marks and capital letters where they are needed.
Add an ending to the story.

Be Careful What You Wish for

Robert heard someone calling his name. He looked all around He could not see anyone. He was all alone on the sidewalk. All of his friends had gone inside to start their homework or have dinner. He heard someone call him again. Who could it be? He listened carefully. The voice seemed to be coming from inside his bookbag. Robert opened his bookbag and looked inside. There stood a tiny man dressed in a green suit. He was wearing red shoes and a hat with bells on it .

The tiny man said his name was Elvin. He was a magic elf. He told Robert to wish for whatever he wanted. Elvin said he would make the wish come true. Robert thought about ice cream. Zap! There was an ice cream cone in his hand. Robert began to grin. This was going to be great! Robert decided

Endings will vary.

© 1996 Kelley Wingate Publications   90   KW 1203

Worksheet 3 (page 91)

Name_____ Skill: Proof for Capitals and Punctuation

> Sentences need punctuation marks.
> Sentences and proper nouns begin with capital letters.

Place punctuation marks and capital letters where they are needed.
Add an ending to the story.

Tell the Truth

My little sister Penny had a hard time telling the truth. She made up stories all the time. She was always getting herself in trouble. Sometimes she made me a part of her stories and I got in trouble too. My mother told her to stop making up stories. Mother said that Penny's nose would start to grow every time she told a lie. Penny would look just like Pinnochio. Penny just laughed. She did not believe mom.

One day Penny ran into the house. She said that a dinosaur was coming down our street. Penny's nose began to twitch. It

Endings will vary.

© 1996 Kelley Wingate Publications   91   KW 1203

Worksheet 4 (page 92)

Name_____ Skill: Proof for Capitals and Punctuation

> Proofread work to correct punctuation, capitals, and spelling.

The first copy of a story is called a "rough draft". When you read your "rough draft" you may find mistakes. Correct any mistakes then rewrite your "rough draft" as a final copy.

Example: Gary and I went to the store last Monday. We bought candy.

1. Use these lines to write a "rough draft". Proofread your story and correct it.

Stories will vary.

2. Use the corrected "rough draft" to write your final copy below.

Stories will vary.

© 1996 Kelley Wingate Publications   92   KW 1203

© 1996 Kelley Wingate Publications   125   CD-3718

Answer Key

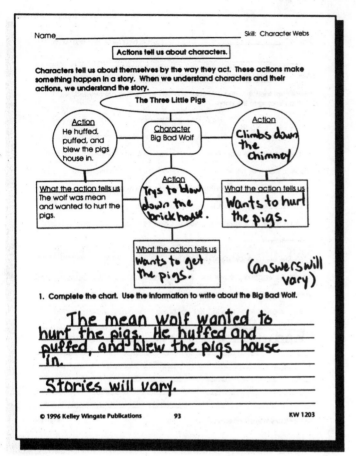

Name_____ Skill: Character Webs

Actions tell us about characters.

Characters tell us about themselves by the way they act. These actions make something happen in a story. When we understand characters and their actions, we understand the story.

The Three Little Pigs

Action
He huffed, puffed, and blew the pigs house in.

Character
Big Bad Wolf

Action
Climbs down the Chimney

Action
Trys to blow down the brick house.

What the action tells us
The wolf was mean and wanted to hurt the pigs.

What the action tells us
Wants to hurt the pigs.

What the action tells us
Wants to get the pigs.

(answers will vary)

1. Complete the chart. Use the information to write about the Big Bad Wolf.

The mean wolf wanted to hurt the pigs. He huffed and puffed, and blew the pigs house in.

Stories will vary.

© 1996 Kelley Wingate Publications   93   KW 1203

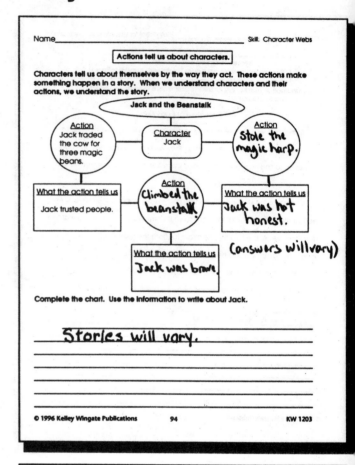

Name_____ Skill: Character Webs

Actions tell us about characters.

Characters tell us about themselves by the way they act. These actions make something happen in a story. When we understand characters and their actions, we understand the story.

Jack and the Beanstalk

Action
Jack traded the cow for three magic beans.

Character
Jack

Action
Stole the magic harp.

Action
Climbed the beanstalk.

What the action tells us
Jack trusted people.

What the action tells us
Jack was not honest.

What the action tells us
Jack was brave.

(answers will vary)

Complete the chart. Use the information to write about Jack.

Stories will vary.

© 1996 Kelley Wingate Publications   94   KW 1203

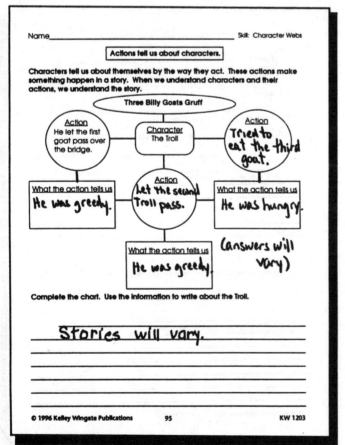

Name_____ Skill: Character Webs

Actions tell us about characters.

Characters tell us about themselves by the way they act. These actions make something happen in a story. When we understand characters and their actions, we understand the story.

Three Billy Goats Gruff

Action
He let the first goat pass over the bridge.

Character
The Troll

Action
Tried to eat the third goat.

Action
Let the second Troll pass.

What the action tells us
He was greedy.

What the action tells us
He was hungry.

What the action tells us
He was greedy.

(answers will vary)

Complete the chart. Use the information to write about the Troll.

Stories will vary.

© 1996 Kelley Wingate Publications   95   KW 1203

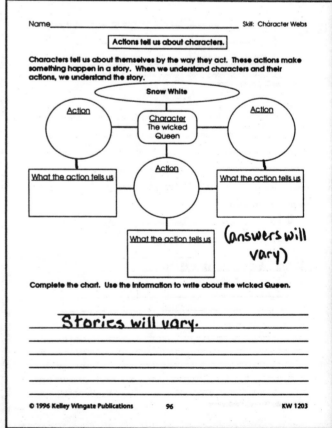

Name_____ Skill: Character Webs

Actions tell us about characters.

Characters tell us about themselves by the way they act. These actions make something happen in a story. When we understand characters and their actions, we understand the story.

Snow White

Action

Character
The wicked Queen

Action

Action

What the action tells us

What the action tells us

What the action tells us

(answers will vary)

Complete the chart. Use the information to write about the wicked Queen.

Stories will vary.

© 1996 Kelley Wingate Publications   96   KW 1203

Answer Key

Name_____ Skill: Character Webs

Actions tell us about characters.

Characters tell us about themselves by the way they act. These actions make something happen in a story. When we understand characters and their actions, we understand the story.

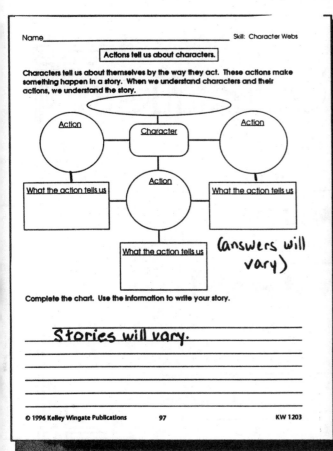

(answers will vary)

Complete the chart. Use the information to write your story.

Stories will vary.
_____
_____
_____
_____

© 1996 Kelley Wingate Publications   97   KW 1203

Name _____ Skill: Book Reports

Book Report

Title: Reports will vary.

Author:

1. Name two characters in this book. Write a sentence about each one.

1. _____
   _____
2. _____
   _____

2. Tell where this story takes place. Write a sentence to describe the setting.
_____
_____

3. What is the problem in this story?
_____
_____
_____

4. How is the problem solved?
_____
_____
_____

© 1996 Kelley Wingate Publications   98   KW 1203

Skill: Book Reports

About This Book

Name _____

Characters

Reports will vary.
(title)
By:
(author)

(end)

(middle)

(beginning)

© 1996 Kelley Wingate Publications   99   KW 1203

Name _____ Skill: Book Reports

Book Review

Title: Reports will vary.

Author: _____

1. Retell the story in your own words. Be sure to include the characters, setting, beginning, middle, and end.
_____
_____
_____
_____
_____
_____
_____

2. What did you like most about this book? Tell why and use examples from the book.
_____
_____
_____
_____
_____
_____
_____

© 1996 Kelley Wingate Publications   100   KW 1203

You are Terrific!

_____

receives this award for

_____

Keep up the great work!

_____   _____

signed   date

Subtraction Superstar!

_____

is a Subtraction Superstar!

_____

I am Proud of YOU!

_____   _____

signed   date

Master Multiplyer!

_____

receives this award for

_____

Keep up the great work!

_____   _____

signed   date

Subtraction Superstar!

_____

is a Subtraction Superstar!

_____

You are terrific!

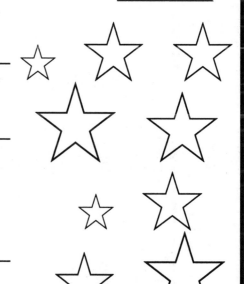

_____   _____

signed   date

129   CD-3718

Great Success!

_____

earns this award for

_____

I am Proud of You!

_____ Signed

_____ Date

astronaut	again	address	about
beginning	basketball	baseball	autumn
buy	bottom	birthday	best
capital	candy	camel	cactus

chest	chase	catcher	careful
cross	crater	crack	classroom
dinner	detail	desk	darkness
easy	early	during	dock

favorite	garden	head	late
excite	front	hamburger	kisses
envelope	friend	hair	hungry
end	fireman	great	homework

main	ocean	period	present
lunch	month	path	pour
lightening	money	party	pool
leash	middle	order	pick

reason	rather	race	quiet
sent	seed	scary	rinse
smell	skunk	shower	shopping
storm	stood	spring	spray

sunlight	toast	wishbone	wisk
student	thunder	water	web
street	terrible	visit	write
strange	table	total	wonderful